KILLERS

JAMES MCCLURE is the author of several highly praised novels including *The Steam Pig*, which won a Gold Dagger award. His latest book, *Rogue Eagle*, will be published in August 1976. He began his career as a crime and court reporter in South Africa, covering every sort of case from shoplifting to murder and treason, but now lives in Oxford where, between novels, he pursues a lifelong interest in British murder trials.

CLIVE EXTON, who wrote the 'Killers' television scripts, first attracted attention with his play *No Fixed Abode* in 1958. He was part of the team that produced 'Armchair Theatre' in the early sixties, and went on to write such diverse screenplays as 'Night Must Fall', 'Isadora', 'Entertaining Mr Sloane', and 'Ten Rillington Place'. He is currently working on 'The Crezz', a twelve-play series for Thames Television, a new film and his first novel.

THE KILLERS ON THE COVER ARE...

Top

Patrick Herbert Mahon, Sidney Harry Fox
Alfred Arthur Rouse,

Bottom

St......... M........, Thomas John Ley

JAMES McCLURE

Killers

A companion to the Thames Television series by

CLIVE EXTON

FONTANA/Collins

First published by Fontana Books 1976

© Clive Exton and Sabenska Gakalu Limited 1976

Made and printed in Great Britain by
William Collins Sons & Co Ltd Glasgow

For 'Bill' W. S. Naude
a remarkable detective

CONTENTS

This book is based on five famous murder trials which, if reproduced in full, would alone make it seven inches thick.

So obviously it's going to contain a lot less than was heard over that total of 33 suspenseful days, But, in another way, it will contain a lot more.

Because no British trial ever attempts (and that is the operative word) to reveal the whole story. Besides being impracticable, the rules of evidence forbid the introduction of anything that can't be shown to bear directly on the matter in question, however much a part of the overall picture it may appear to be.

Of course, like all theories, this one is subject to exceptions and contradictions, as we shall see; yet the effect is still to isolate a trial from reality, as it were – and to leave some of the most intriguing questions unanswered.

One of the things this book tries to do is to give each trial its context by providing a 'before and after', and by placing it in a certain sequence. Another is to supply answers to those questions where possible, or to use the facts to suggest probable explanations.

But as to what *really* happened in each of these five cases, that remains up to you – and this is where the fascination lies. There's nothing cut and dried about them; instead, there is plenty of scope for imagination, deduction and your very own, personal opinion.

This book, for example, takes the view that Steinie Morrison was convicted largely because of misguided zeal on the part of his counsel. Whereas Clive Exton, who devised and wrote the superb television series that the book accompanies, totally and cheerfully disagrees with this interpretation. In his opinion' Morrison's counsel simply took every means open to him to secure an acquittal, concentrating the attack on the character of the prosecution witnesses.

The fact that two such different views can co-exist about the same trial, without rancour on either side, should encourage you to make up your own mind about Steinie Morrison – and the others. Incidentally, it is also a tribute to the generosity of spirit shown by Mr Exton, the senior partner in this joint venture; a lesser man might have declared his own interpretation to be the only one.

To begin then, easing in gently with the least puzzling, most grisly murder of the five . . .

Chapter One

THE CRUMBLES MURDER

REX *v*. PATRICK HERBERT MAHON

JULY 1924

Animal magnetism is common among lady-killers, or so the more gallant Press would have us believe – while overlooking how unflattering the corollary must be for the ladies it defends.

But this does seem to have been literally true of Patrick Herbert Mahon: all sorts of creatures were drawn to him in a most unusual way. Frequently he would arrive back at his boarding house with other people's loyal pets, which had tagged along uninvited, and he would delight his friends by whistling wild birds down out of the trees. Perhaps it was simply that animals could recognize the beast in him.

Which isn't as fanciful or as forgiving as it might sound. There is, however, something ridiculous about the repeated gasps over how 'callous' he was in committing a particularly revolting murder and, in the same bated breath, bedding a new woman with only his selfish needs in view. One might as well start calling any domesticated predator, which mixes gruesome acts of survival with moments of sexual frolic, an unfeeling son of a bitch – and very few dog-lovers would take kindly to that.

Plain Herbert Mahon was born to a large Liverpool-Irish family in 1890; a family which kept its grip on the lower rung of the middle class by placing its faith in diligence, sportsmanship and God. He appeared to respond well to the demands made upon him, and soon endeared himself in every quarter with his puppylike energy, appealing looks and eagerness to please.

After leaving school, where his brightness and athletic prowess earned special mention, he was first an office boy and soon a junior clerk. He maintained an interest in French (which he spoke fluently) and in Latin (which he liked to quote), attended worship regularly, and played football in the local church league.

But he was not altogether the conformist that these rather

9

superficial facts would seem to indicate.

This first became apparent when Herbert, as his frugal parents had him christened, helped himself to a second name. Patrick, he felt, went much better with Mahon; it also allowed him to encourage his acquaintances to call him Pat, which was undoubtedly a more short caressing form than Herb or Bert.

Clearly, Mahon himself decided what sort of man he wanted to be, and altered things accordingly. For a foretaste of that cultivated image at its prime, there's the blarney-laden entry he made beside his name in a bowls club register: 'A Broth of a Bhoy, who deserved to be born at sea.'

His early independence showed itself in other ways as well. The most startling for his parents was the proposal of marriage he put to his school-days sweetheart when she was only sixteen. This didn't much amuse her parents either, and both families opposed the match on the grounds of the couple's extreme youth.

Two years later, however, the persuasive Mahon and his dark-haired, very capable bride were setting up home in Liverpool. He had needed her, and having got her, the long chase down the straight and narrow had ended.

And so, within a matter of months, he decided to go in pursuit of someone else. He and the girl ran away together to the Isle of Man, but there Mahon was arrested for financing the flight by forging and uttering cheques worth £123 of his firm's money.

Back in Liverpool, the first offender's luck improved. He was merely bound over, and Mrs Mahon, believing he had come to heel, forgave him. They then agreed to start all over again from the beginning, preferably somewhere else.

The Mahons settled in Wiltshire. He found a job with a dairy, and all went well for a time. Mahon's business acumen was considerable, his colleagues liked him, and his skill as a footballer won him general popularity.

However, shortly after Mrs Mahon had given birth to a daughter, the new father was jailed for a year, having embezzled £60 belonging to the dairy.

That was a formative year for Mahon: he made a number of unusual friends, and learned a thing or two, behind those prison walls.

Burglary could have been one of them. There was a series of unsolved raids round about Calne in Wiltshire after his release. And Mahon, who had been living there, moved on.

Surrey was his next stop. He started working for a dairy at Sunningdale and, possibly with fresh resolve, kept his fingers out of the till. But he couldn't keep his hands off the women.

Fired for scandalous behaviour and thrown back on his own resources, Mahon tried to scrape a living from odd jobs at race meetings, helped by the contacts he'd made in prison. On really good days, he'd act as a bookmaker's clerk. On bad days, he'd have the law after him or not make a thing.

Mahon had experienced quite a few of those bad days by the beginning of 1916, and this drove him to commit his first major crime.

He bungled it in an extraordinary fashion.

His target was the Sunningdale branch of the National Provincial Bank. He managed to break in successfully after dark, but was surprised by a maidservant from the floor above. Mahon reacted instinctively, attacking her with a hammer so that she fell stunned.

When the maid recovered her senses, Mahon was still there. He had her in his arms, and was kissing and stroking her gently, while reassuring her most charmingly that he'd never meant her any real harm. He was so anxious she should think no ill of him, that it didn't occur to her that his attentions were anything other than honourable; it was, in fact, rather like being licked by a penitent big dog.

Whatever the lasting impression he made on her, it was certainly a vivid one. Assisted by an excellent description, the police arrested Mahon in another town, and he appeared for trial at Guildford Assizes.

Sweet talk was wasted on Mr Justice Darling, as Mahon – with his sensitivity for names – should have guessed.

He tried it all the same. And when the jury returned their verdict of 'guilty', the prisoner begged to be allowed to join the army and do his stuff for dear old England.

The army had no need of hypocrites, he was told, before being sent down for five years.

But what irony there was in that mawkish little scene: asking to serve at the Front in 1916 was tantamount to inviting a death sentence, and that was something Mahon would try anything to avoid when next he faced a judge.

The Crumbles says it all. Two miles of unlovely shingle, stretching from Eastbourne to Wallsend on Pevensey Bay, a mile across at its widest point, skirted by a road and some coarse, dusty undergrowth, and valued only as a source of railway ballast in the year 1920.

Except by humble young holidaymakers like Irene Munro, a poorly-dressed typist of 17 down from London, for whom the uninterrupted vista it provided must have been 'heaven' – as, no doubt, some of them wrote on their postcards home. One hopes Miss Munro didn't: that would have been altogether too horribly apt.

Her body was found on the Crumbles five days after her arrival in Eastbourne. A blood-stained stone lay nearby, and her head had also been struck by a stick which had left the imprint of a carved bulldog. Her handbag, which her landlady had seen to contain holiday money, was empty.

A murder hunt began.

Other visitors remembered seeing a girl in green walking with two youngish men, one of whom had been wearing a herring-bone suit.

So the Eastbourne police stopped and questioned anyone in a herring-bone suit. William Gray, 29, answered the description, and he was taken into custody for two days with his companion, 19-year-old Jack Field, another idler. But they were released for want of any evidence against them, and were able to return to their life of leisure.

Until the investigating officers received an odd piece of information from the recruiting station in the town. It then appeared that, within minutes of the grim discovery on the shingle, both men had made urgent applications to join the army.

From there on, the rest was fairly simple: a barmaid recalled the pair being penniless on the morning of the murder, but flush in the evening; and a labourer, who knew Gray, said he'd seen him walking with a young couple towards the Crumbles on the same day.

Gray and Field were tried before Mr Justice Avory at Lewes Assizes on December 13, where they denied having any part in the murder. The jury thought otherwise, and the executions were carried out at Wandsworth, with each man finally blaming the other for the killing before the gallows cut short their argument.

The trial was memorable in itself for Gray's nonchalance. After being advised against giving evidence by his eminent counsel, Mr Edward Marshall-Hall, the accused dozed off. This was not mistaken for the sound sleep of the just, however, and the judge reprimanded him severely.

But there were other reasons the trial was to be remembered when, some four years later, Mr Justice Avory again presided over a murder trial at Lewes.

One reason was that the Irene Munro case introduced Sir Bernard Spilsbury, the Home Office Pathologist, to the Crumbles. He was called in only to verify the findings of two post-mortems on the body, and did not give evidence at the trial himself. (Spilsbury's conclusions were that Miss Munro had probably taken 30 minutes to die, through the combined effects of shock, loss of blood, and asphyxia caused by the weight of shingle on her chest.) Yet this brief visit did establish for him a link with the scene of what he would come to regard as his greatest triumph.

And then there was the remark made on Gray's behalf by Marshall-Hall. 'I am not suggesting that murders go on there,' he told a witness, after asking if the Crumbles wasn't held to be a sinister sort of place.

These can't be called prophetic words exactly. Neither can they be dismissed as having nothing to do with the really uncanny elements in the downfall of Patrick Herbert Mahon.

Who was about to be released again.

Many people would have given up the struggle long before Mrs Mahon first showed any sign of weakening. That five-year sentence must have been a dreadful jolt for her, but there was worse to follow. The son she had in 1916 died without living long enough to see his father.

Mother and daughter moved to London, not expecting much, although willing to believe that their fortune might still change for the better. And it did.

Not long after Mrs Mahon succeeded in securing a lowly position with Consols Automatic Aerators Ltd., which had a factory at Sunbury-on-Thames, her exceptional efficiency caught the management's attention. They were so impressed by her that she was promoted to company secretary.

This meant that when Mahon came out of prison, as contrite as ever, and promising to mend his ways for good, his wife was able to use her influence in getting him on to the staff. It was a calculated risk – nobody was informed of his criminal record – but one which seemed more than likely to come off.

Mahon made the most of this opportunity, and rapidly earned the reputation of being one of the firm's best travelling salesmen. He doesn't appear to have neglected the domestic side of his life either; the family settled into a flat in Kew, built up a new circle of friends, and prospered.

Then in May, 1922, came a threat to everything Mrs Mahon had worked for: the soda-fountain company was placed in the hands of a receiver, because of some action taken by a debenture holder, and their jobs seemed suddenly in jeopardy. Her relief can be imagined when she found out that not only was she to carry on her normal duties, but that her husband had actually been promoted to sales manager at £750 a year.

And yet, tragically, that receivership did in fact signal the end of her hard-won happiness – if in a somewhat roundabout way.

A year passed. Mr Hobbins, the chartered accountant appointed as receiver in control of Consols Automatic, and the man who'd chosen Mahon to be his deputy now, as manager, engaged a new shorthand-typist.

Miss Emily Bealby Kaye was 37 years old, and lived at the Green Cross Club for 'bachelor girls' in Guilford Street, Bloomsbury. Like Irene Munro, she'd herself been a typist at 17, having lost the security of a comfortably-off middle-class home when both her parents died suddenly. This early and traumatic change in her circumstances probably accounted for her thriftiness, and by 1923 she had accumulated a reasonable nest egg. Miss Kaye was bright, practical and even-tempered, and consequently fitted in well at the club. But Miss Kaye wasn't much to look at. She was tall, according to some descriptions, with the big build of a hearty woman athlete. Her face was sweet enough and her chin firm, only her nose was so noticeably large that unkind comparisons with party novelties become almost unavoidable.

She wore her fair hair bobbed, and used a string of beads to accentuate her very long neck.

A neck she laid on the block the day a handsome young businessman came to call on Mr Hobbins. The visitor was expensively dressed and possessed of a charming manner. He had deep-set, merry eyes, a wide dimpled smile, neat pointed ears, a high forehead, and curly fair hair with a natural quiff. A face one might find today in the stills from an old pot-boiler Western, or fronting an evangelical mission on the doorsteps of suburbia.

Miss Kaye fell in love with this man, who called on Mr Hobbins fairly often, and sometimes she discussed business matters on the telephone with his wife.

The Mahons moved to a boarding house in Pagoda Road, Richmond, during January, 1924. An expedient move, it would seem, because Mrs Mahon was now beginning to find her high standards as a company secretary took their toll, and this at least spared her the problems of running a home. She and her husband continued to be a much-sought-after couple at various functions, and, to her delight, he was elected honorary secretary of the bowls club. All was still going just as she'd hoped and prayed.

Mrs Mahon did, however, begin to wonder about this as spring approached and her husband seemed to be away on business rather a lot. Her uneasiness turned to nagging worry, and, when added to the burden of pressure under which she'd worked for so long, it made Mrs Mahon ill. She didn't leave Consols Automatic though; that job was far too precious to her and her picturebook daughter.

April brought a really bewildering sequence of appearances and disappearances. Over two weekends, Mahon sent his wife telegrams from three different places, each with a message intended to explain his absence, but only making it more puzzling.

And then Mrs Mahon, who'd presumably asked around to see if anyone knew what was happening, heard something that made her despair: her husband had been seen on Easter Saturday at the Plumpton races.

She did nothing until Mahon went off for the third weekend running. Then, almost certain he was up to his old Sunning-dale tricks again, she started to search through his large wardrobe of clothes for some clue to the reason for his mysterious behaviour. A betting stub would have confirmed her worst suspicions, but all she could come up with was a cloakroom ticket from Waterloo Station.

Mrs Mahon clutched at this straw. On the following Thursday – which was also May Day – she went to ask a friend's help. The former railway policeman took the ticket and promised to make a discreet inquiry.

A promise he found impossible to keep, once he'd claimed the locked Gladstone bag and had taken a look inside it, by pulling open the ends.

Scotland Yard took over. A detective was placed on watch at the cloakroom counter, and the ticket was returned to Mrs Mahon. Reassured to hear that the bag's contents had no connection with bookmaking – which is all that was said to her – she replaced the ticket in Mahon's coat pocket, and made no mention of the incident when he came home that night.

The next morning Mrs Mahon went to hospital, and learned that she'd have to undergo surgery.

At about 6.15 that evening, Mahon went to Waterloo Station, collected his bag, and was stopped on his way out by a detective.

'Rubbish!' snapped Mahon, on being warned that he was to be taken to Kennington Road police station.

Chief Inspector Percy Savage interviewed him there briefly at 8.30 p.m. and, after hearing that the key to the bag had been 'lost', suggested a move to his own offices at Scotland Yard.

'All right,' said Mahon, more amenably.

An hour later, the contents of the bag were placed before him: two pieces of new silk, a pair of torn twill bloomers, a towel, a silk scarf, a cook's knife, and a tennis racquet cover with the initials *E.B.K.* on it. All these items were covered in blood, and the inside of the bag was heavily sprinkled with Sanitas disinfectant.

Mahon was asked how they had come into his possession.

'I am fond of dogs – I must have carried meat for the dogs in it.'

'That will not do,' said Chief Inspector Savage. 'These stains are of human blood.'

'You seem to know all about it!' Mahon retorted.

Then followed a very curious confrontation: for a whole quarter of an hour, nobody said a word.

'I wonder,' the prisoner asked, 'if you can realize how terrible a thing it is for one's body to be active and one's mind fail to act.'

That was all. He fell silent again for 30 minutes.

'I am considering my position,' he informed his inter-rogators.

They made no response, and another quarter of an hour dragged by. The tension was now close to being unbearable.

'I suppose you know everything,' he said at last. 'I will tell you the truth.'

And, having been cautioned, he began to make the first of three statements. It took him until 2.30 on Saturday morning; he collapsed once and had to be revived with a stimulant. At 4 a.m. he started talking again, but by then Chief Inspector Savage was already on his way to the Crumbles – and to the most dreadful sight he'd ever seen.

The whole story of Mahon's secret affair with Miss Emily Bealby Kaye – whom he called 'Peter' – was supposedly revealed in those three horrifying statements.

He had met Miss Kaye, Mahon said, about ten months earlier while she was working for Mr Hobbins. They had also often spoken on the telephone together. One day, towards the end of summer, she'd suggested a day on the river.

'. . . as I was anxious to gain some impartial knowledge of the legal proceedings in connection with the litigation in which the company was concerned, I accepted.

'We spent the afternoon at Staines, and Miss Kaye was extremely affectionate, and among other things, told me she was particularly fond of me and wished to be friendly.

'Intimacy (friendliness indeed) took place on that occasion; as a result I realized she was a woman of the world, which knowledge came as rather a surprise to me.

'Subsequently I met Miss Kaye, of course, from time to time in the course of my duties, and by her request met her on many occasions by appointment when we had lunch etc. Intimacy took place on several other occasions.'

Just before Christmas, Miss Kaye had been dismissed by Mr Hobbins because of some staff rearrangements and this had left her with time on her hands – time to become more demanding.

'I felt sorry for the fact she had been dismissed and did, as a result, meet her a bit more frequently.

'I temporized in the hope of gaining time, but from that moment I felt more or less at the mercy of a strong-minded woman whom, although I liked her in many ways, I did not tremendously care for.'

Miss Kaye's next job had been with a financier in Bond Street. This had encouraged her to speculate in francs, and to have Mahon take a fifty-fifty share in the gamble. Miss Kaye had handed him £100 notes to be cashed and shared at various times; he had signed these with false names for fear 'she might have some ulterior motive' in not going to the bank herself.

'After losing her job with the financier in Bond Street (Miss Kaye had been filling in for someone away ill), she became thoroughly unsettled and begged me to give up everything and go abroad with her. She informed me of her great love and affection for me, but I plainly told her I could not agree to such a course.'

Then Miss Kaye had outlined what they were to call their 'love experiment':

'. . . she suggested I should take a holiday and go away with her for a week or two, and take a bungalow where we could be alone together, and where she would convince me with her love that I could be perfectly happy with her.'

Mahon had resisted this idea until the last day in March, when he met Miss Kaye for tea at Waterloo Station after her return from Bournemouth, where she had been recuperating from a bout of 'flu.

'She startled me with the information that she had written to the club secretary giving up her rooms, and that she was determined to force an issue somehow.

'She suggested plans I did agree with, and I reminded her of the fact that I could not in decency break the pledge I had given my business friends to keep things going at the works until the litigation was finally settled.'

(That sentence appears to contain a Freudian error in the first line, and the copies of this statement used in court read: 'She suggested plans I did *not* agree with . . .' But, as Mahon had signed the original, after checking it, the phrasing had to stand, much to the embarrassment of the defence, which was caught unawares by the typist's mistake.)

'She however persisted, and ultimately I agreed, feeling it was my best course if only to gain time to consider the suggestion.'

On the Friday Miss Kaye had telephoned Mahon and drawn his attention to an advertisement for a bungalow at Langney, near Eastbourne. He'd gone down there the following morning, seen a Mr Muir, and had taken the bungalow for two months.

Mahon's reasons for the long tenancy varied. In one place he said: 'I felt convinced that the experiment which Miss Kaye had suggested – that is a few days alone in which to gain my affection – would not succeed.' In another he stated, after a reference to his wife's pending operation: 'I thought if I took the bungalow it would be a nice surprise for her.'

Miss Kaye had been 'roused to fury' over the two-month let – the implication being that she'd expected to snare him far sooner – but she had gone down to inspect the property for herself all the same.

This visit had changed everything, and she had enthused over his choice from her hotel in Eastbourne.

'Her last words to me on the phone were: "Pat, old boy, you'll never regret it, as I can make up fully for all you may have to give up".'

'I felt in myself very depressed and miserable, and did not want to spend the three or four days together as she desired, but as I had given my word, and as I felt that I could definitely prove during that time to Miss Kaye how foolish the hope it was on her part to expect to keep my affection, even if she could gain it, I thought I had better go through with it.'

'I travelled down to Eastbourne on the Friday, 11th (of April), saw Mr Muir at the bungalow and obtained the keys, informing him my wife (Miss Kaye) would be down the next day.'

Mahon had then gone back to London, where he was needed at the Sunbury factory to deal with some problem, and had returned on Saturday morning with his kitbag.

'Miss Kaye was charmed with the place and told me again that she knew she was going to succeed in her object. To my mind this object was now an idea fixed, almost an obsession in her mind.'

Her last weekend had been spent very quietly. Miss Kaye had done some cooking and cleaning, and Monday had passed in much the same way.

But Tuesday had begun with a row at the breakfast table; she had wanted to discuss their 'immediate plans' and he hadn't. A little later on, however, he had promised to apply for a passport, and they'd gone up to London. There she had gone off alone to see some friends.

Miss Kaye now had only hours to live.

'We travelled back to Eastbourne and, on the way, the whole question was re-opened and I informed her that I had not been for the passport, and did not intend to do so.

'We quarrelled and had heated words, but eventually arrived at the bungalow more or less in calm mood.

'Soon after arrival, Miss Kaye – having taken off her coat and hat – suddenly startled me with the expression on her face, which appeared to be extremely determined.'

Her next move had been to sit down and start writing letters which would commit them both to a 'definite line of action'.

'She also asked me to write to the Assistant Secretary of a function (the Richmond bowls tournament) of which I am Honorary Secretary, stating that I was giving up the work, and stating also that we were going overland to Paris for a time, and then on to South Africa.

'I refused absolutely to write such a letter, and felt that matters had come by now to a crisis. She, however, fumed and raged and finally wrote the note herself and begged me to sign it; again I refused.'

Mahon had not agreed to the next demand she made, which concerned writing a letter of a similar nature to his friends.

'This appeared to anger Miss Kaye beyond endurance and she suddenly picked up a weapon – an axe – a coal axe – and threw it at me; it struck me on the shoulder and glanced off and hit the door, breaking the shaft.

'Then I saw red,' Mahon said in his first statement. 'We fought and struggled. She was a very big strong girl. She appeared to be quite mad with anger and rage.'

In his second statement Mahon said: 'I felt appalled at the fury she showed and realized suddenly how strong the girl was. She followed up the throw by dashing at me and clutching at my face and neck.

'In sheer desperation and fright, I closed with her, doing my best to fight back and loosen her hold. We struggled and eventually, in the course of the struggle, we fell over an easy chair and Miss Kaye's head came into violent contact with the round coal cauldron . . .

'My body of course being on top when she fell, her hold relaxed a bit and she lay apparently stunned or dead.

'The events of the next few seconds I cannot remember except as a nightmare of horror, for I saw blood beginning to ooze from Miss Kaye's head where she had struck the cauldron.

'I did my utmost to revive her, and I simply could not at the time say whether I strangled her or whether she died of the fall; but from the moment she fell and struck her head, she did not move.

'By this time, the excitement of the struggle and the fright and the blows I had received, had reduced me to a condition of nervous exhaustion.'

Mahon had gone into the garden in 'a state bordering on madness', but had returned later to place her body 'gently' in the second bedroom before spending the night in East-bourne.

Two days later – Thursday, April 17 – he had gone to London, where he'd bought a knife and a saw from a 'Staines' shop in Victoria Street.

'When I got back to Langney I was still so upset and worried that I could not then carry out my intention to decapitate the body.

'I did so on Good Friday. I severed the legs from the hips, the head, and left the arms on. I then put the various parts in a trunk which I locked up. I left the trunk in the bedroom and locked the door.'

Mahon had locked the door because he was expecting a guest to arrive at about lunch-time. She was a Miss Duncan whom he'd met some six weeks before in Richmond – 'a woman down on her luck, not a prostitute'.

His explanation for this was that when 'the realization of the whole thing dawned on me', it had struck him that the 'damn place' was haunted.

'I thought: I can't get the wife down – if I do, she will find the body. I got this girl, the one I met at Richmond – I thought I was doing her a good turn – down to the bungalow.'

21

And he added: 'I should have gone stark raving mad if I had not had her with me. It was ghastly.'

Miss Duncan, who'd received £4 wired to her by Mahon on the Thursday, had done some cleaning for him.

'She came down on Good Friday and went back on Easter Monday (accompanied by Mahon). I never confided in her as to what had happened. She saw feminine articles about, and I told her my wife was down.'

Mahon had treated Miss Duncan to dinner in London, and then had taken her home. On Tuesday he'd been able to return to the bungalow as the works at Sunbury were still closed.

'I burnt the head in an ordinary fire; it was finished in three hours. The poker went through the head when I poked it. The next day I broke the skull and put the pieces in the dustbin. The thigh bone I burned. It is surprising what a room fire will burn.'

After dealing with the skull, he had been obliged to make an appearance at work.

'I went down to Langney again on Friday night, 25th April, and stayed at the 'Sussex' or 'Clifton' Hotel that night, going over to the bungalow about 10 o'clock on Saturday morning, the 26th April.

'I had to cut up the trunk; I also cut off the arms. I burned portions of them, the smell was appalling, and I had to think of some other method of disposing of the portions.

'I then boiled some portions in a large pot in the bungalow, cut up the portions small, packed them in the brown bag, and I threw them out of the train whilst I was travelling between Waterloo and Richmond; these portions were not wrapped in anything; this was about 10 o'clock on Sunday, 27th April.'

Then Mahon corrected himself: he'd actually been compelled to journey on to Reading, 'as I could not dispose of all the portions between Waterloo and Richmond.'

He had stayed overnight at a Reading hotel, and the bag had been left at Waterloo Station to await his planned return on Friday night to 'get some more flesh'.

For the dogs and other scavengers which were helping him remove every trace of his crime.

There was a ring of truth about much of what Mahon said in those statements. And the one obvious lie wasn't his own:

this was when he gave Miss Kaye's age as 29 – she was, in fact, in her 39th year.

The nearest thing to a written record of her side of the story was the small number of letters she sent friends and relatives about this time.

Her married sister, who'd had her to stay at the New Year, had received a note during Miss Kaye's convalescence in Bournemouth. The note had told her that Emily was now engaged to 'Pat Derek Patterson', and that he wanted his fiancé to go with him to South Africa, where he had a 'good post' in Cape Town.

Miss Kaye had also written to her again on April 5 (immediately after Mahon had first contacted Mr Muir about the bungalow), to say that they would be off in ten days.

According to Mahon, exactly ten days later Miss Kaye had departed this life.

A similar irony was to be found in the letter which she'd written to a former room-mate of hers at the Green Cross Club; it had been dated the day before her death, and was on notepaper taken from the Kenilworth Court Hotel in Eastbourne:

Dear Old Phiz:

Very many thanks for sending on the parcel. Apparently you're up in Town this weekend. I wonder if Fred is up with you. Pat arrived intact, but his arm in a sling, on Saturday and we are having a very nice time; quiet, but a nice change from Town. He particularly wants to get to Paris for Easter and would like you and Fred to come and have dinner with us when we return to Town, which we shall have to do in about a fortnight before setting out on our final journey. This will probably suit you both better too, at any rate I hope so and shall look forward to seeing you then. Any news? We are returning from here Wednesday and go straight over to Paris. Gay old Paris. All news when we meet. Love to all my pals at the Club and lots to yourself, old thing.

Yours ever,
Peter

P.S. If any more letters or anything should come will you send them to me c/o Poste Restante, G.P.O. Paris? Hope you have a good Easter.

Obviously, Miss Kaye was confident of her relationship with Mahon at this stage, whatever his own reservations or deceits. And the fact that she told her sister his name was 'Pat Derek Patterson' underlines her willingness to lie in order to achieve her end. There can be little doubt that this ageing and not very appetizing spinster wasn't going to give up her 'handsome brute of a man' without a fight.

Neither was she going to suffer any scruples about absconding with Mrs Mahon's husband – nor, indeed, with Miss Mahon's father, which means she was prepared to consider two lives as less important than her own. It wasn't as if she'd never come in contact with Mrs Mahon; a few casual inquiries, to check out any sob story Mahon might have told her, could have been fairly easily made.

Miss Kaye had the benefit of a good deal of posthumous sympathy, which cast her as an innocent maid betrayed by the wiles of an Irish charmer. This is a lot of nonsense. She deserves sympathy simply as the sad, silly, slightly desperate figure so often found at the lonely point on a triangle. The rare and really loving disengage themselves before anyone else gets hurt. The rest have to cope with varying degrees of self-interest, and with fantasies which can all too readily deny reality – along with all the danger signals only reality can present.

This denial of the *real* situation is evident in Mahon's references to their quarrels. In one place he says he can't run away with her because of a promise he made to his business colleagues to see Consols through its troubles – a fatuous excuse, but quite in keeping with the classical pattern. In another, their elopement is to be announced to a bowls tournament organizer – an obvious choice as the next most important person in his life, yet just as absurd.

On top of this, Miss Kaye was described by her former room-mate as being 'a strong-minded woman and capable of very deep feeling' – a combination which Mahon, accustomed to easy prey, very likely found surprisingly difficult to handle. And one must always remember that he hated anyone to think ill of him.

His claim that intimacy took place on their first outing has a strong whiff of character assassination about it. But this just could have been true. Miss Kaye hadn't always lived cloistered in the Green Cross Club, but had moved there from a flat in Soho. Perhaps she had been a 'woman of the world' for long enough to miss all the eligible young men, who insisted on virtue in their wives, if not in themselves. Instant intimacy does have a way of making up for lost time, lost youth and lost opportunity.

So much for conjecture – well, almost. Because there is still the question of her confidence: on what was it based?

Superintendent Carlin of Scotland Yard, who made a study of Mahon, once said: 'He was keenly disposed to philandering or having affairs with this or that woman casually as they attracted him. But he never, I am convinced, wished to sever [*sic*] his connection with the domestic hearth.

'He felt in his own mind that the woman he had married was his sheet anchor; that, if he cast off from her, he would be adrift.'

From that one can assume Mahon either told some terrible lies – or that he just went along with things, as he said – and she was stupid enough to believe in his words.

Yet this begs another question: what sort of attraction *did* Miss Kaye have for him? Or was it something far more than that which locked them into a prolonged and calamitous liaison?

It could have been her £700 nest egg – although there were plenty of other susceptible women about, much better off.

It could have been sexual – the jaded Mahon may have become kinky, but nothing is novel forever.

It could have been the child beginning to grow in Miss Kaye's womb – but this would surely have been a source of acute anxiety, rather than of buoyant confidence, until he had actually 'married' her. (And besides, there is no positive proof that either of them knew about this pregnancy, which was still in its very early stages.)

It might have been the first of those three strange coincidences which contributed to his damnation. This was when, according to Edgar Wallace at his most responsible, Miss Kaye chanced across a court report while clearing out a drawer – presumably at the Green Cross Club – lined with an old newspaper. From it she had learned Mahon's closely-kept secret: that five-year sentence for the Sunningdale bank fiasco. Just a word or two in the ear of Mr Hobbins at the office and . . .

There is something about this particular coincidence

which worries one a bit – the other two being authenticated beyond dispute. It does, however, suggest a most plausible answer to the question.

Such knowledge could, if used to unfair advantage, inspire confidence in someone with designs like Miss Kaye; just as it could inspire someone else to cut them up into very small pieces.

One piece of large intestine found on Sunday, May 4, was eight inches long.

Once, while Sir Bernard Spilsbury was giving a talk to the Cambridge University Medical Society, what he said made a listener scream, throw a fit and bite the chairman's thumb. Others fainted.

So when he described the remains of Miss Kaye as being the most gruesome he'd ever encountered, that was saying something.

It was also paying an oblique compliment to the widow in a fur coat who accompanied him to Eastbourne that weekend. Mrs Bainbridge had applied for a job at his hospital after her husband, a former professor there and a friend of Spilsbury's, had died. She had been appointed to help in the pathology museum but, much as in Mrs Mahon's case, her intelligence and efficiency, coupled with an interest in post-mortem work, had led to rapid promotion as the great man's first secretary. Although her nerve had already been tested in the mortuary, this – her début in a major investigation – could have proved somewhat overwhelming. Yet Mrs Bainbridge stayed at Spilsbury's side, imperturbably taking down his observations, for the whole eight hours they were there.

The bungalow, Spilsbury discovered, was very near to where Irene Munro's foot had been seen sticking out of the shingle by a 13-year-old boy.

It was called the 'Officer's House', having once been part of the defunct Langney Coastguard Station, and there was a wall around the property and the adjoining row of smaller quarters. The bungalow had nine rooms, and was a simple, square structure, with a chimney at each of the four corners of its lopped-off, pitched roof, and postage-stamp windows. Looking at a picture of it today, one is immediately reminded of the easier models that can be made in Lego –

except that nothing in Lego could look quite so gloomily functional or drab.

A considerable crowd of sightseers was waiting in the spring sunshine when Spilsbury and Mrs Bainbridge arrived and went in through the front entrance.

This brought them immediately into the best-furnished of the nine rooms: a lounge papered with a pattern of potted plants. The walls were also decorated with ornamental plates and a great number of pictures in heavy, wooden frames. There was a mirror over the fireplace, and to the right of the grate stood two coal scuttles, one of which was a tinny replica of a cauldron. A settee and assortment of chairs – ranging from cane to Windsor to plain ordinary – provided enough seating for more than half a dozen people, and beneath the window, with its drawn curtains of a floral design, was a small writing desk. Most poignant, though, was a vase of wilting flowers that had been left on a circular, three-legged table almost in the centre of the carpet.

At a glance, everything looked orderly and neat.

Then the police began to show them around. Spilsbury, who had put on his long white apron and rubber gloves, was shocked to see Chief Inspector Savage handling the grisly evidence with his bare hands, and this was to lead to the introduction of the 'murder bag' every force uses today.

The grisly evidence being, in the first instance, a tenon saw which had flesh and human grease on it. There was more of this grease on the metal fender of the fireplace, in a saucepan, in a bath and in a basin. A saucer of solidified fat lay near the cauldron.

In the fireplace was a two-gallon saucepan; beneath its scum of fat was some reddish fluid and a piece of boiled flesh with skin attached to it.

The large fibre trunk in one of the bedrooms had the initials *E.B.K.* on its lid, a fair indication of the contents: the torso of Emily Bealby Kaye, sawn across at the waist and down the middle, making four parts in all. In among them was a biscuit tin filled with various organs – including that length of intestine. And in a hat-box were thirty-seven pieces of flesh, some wrapped in blood-soaked clothing.

Spilsbury had the police move the kitchen table out into the walled yard, and worked there for three hours on the remains. Most probably this was because the light was better –

it could hardly have been anything to do with the dreadful odours. Much to his dismay, Spilsbury's sense of smell, upon which he relied heavily, had begun to fade about four years before. Often, in order to detect a particular odour by contrast, so to speak, he would put down his instruments, go out into the open air, and then rush back into the mortuary to see what difference this made. His handicap was also a source of dismay to others, who had to remain attentive in almost unendurable conditions, while he worked on quite happily, never suggesting a break. Nor would he allow anyone to seek comfort in a cigarette, as one CID officer had cause to remember after an exhumation: Spilsbury politely asked him to refrain, adding, 'I can't smell the smells I want to smell', and then bent down to sniff at the corpse as if it were a 'rose-garden'. His eye-sight, however, was quite extraordinary, and allowed him to make do without a microscope on occasion. He was able to spot the mark of an abortionist's instrument that no one else could see without a lens, and once he correctly diagnosed a spinal disease which was virtually invisible – his finding being checked by someone else using a slide. Not one of his opinions made in this way was ever squashed in court by evidence based on microscopic examination, but, of course, the slightest doubt would have had him at his microscope, too. The instrument was what had given him his initial interest in medical juris-prudence.

This gift of good vision was employed extensively that afternoon. Spilsbury spent almost all of the time on collecting more than 900 fragments of bone from the ashes found in a dustpan and in the bungalow's fireplaces. Many of these fragments were so tiny and dry that they would have turned to dust in less careful fingers.

Outside the garden, the crowd grew to a tremendous size, and the road became jammed with cars. There wasn't much for these spectators to watch, apart from the activities of the police who were searching for skull bones, but the children enjoyed themselves on the shingle. Then, just as the light was fading, a quick glimpse was caught of Spilsbury and Mrs Bainbridge leaving for London, followed by a variety of sinister containers.

Late that night, when Spilsbury had his top-floor mortuary suite at St Bartholomew's Hospital to himself, he went into the preparation room and began what has been called his masterpiece.

A headless corpse had first brought him into the limelight; it had been that of Mrs Crippen, who'd lived for a time in Guilford Street, where the Green Cross Club stood. His own part in the case, important though he made it, had been limited to a section of scar tissue smaller than a matchbox top. Now he was confronted by hundreds of bits and pieces, many a great deal even smaller than that; some cooked, some raw and some pulverized. All of which, theoretically, would go to make up one body.

Spilsbury worked until 6.30 a.m. He attended to his normal duties during the day, and then carried straight on from where he'd left off. He was not simply a pathologist, but a born detective who couldn't read a book on holiday without noting down his medical deductions in the margin. By Tuesday morning, his work was done.

The torso had been reassembled, and the organs were all back in their proper places. Three leg bones had been restored from the pile of brittle bone fragments, one leg had been confirmed missing, and parts of both hands had been juxtaposed. And, apart from the rest of the bone, there was nothing left over.

With the completion of this astounding reconstruction, Spilsbury was not, as one might suppose, then able to state the cause of Miss Kaye's death. But he was able to say how she *hadn't* died – and that was the important thing.

The dogs encouraged to find the missing limb were no help to the police. A leg was discovered on Wimbledon Common, but it wasn't Miss Kaye's. As a matter of dubious interest, unexplained parts of people crop up surprisingly often; Spilsbury examined scores of them during his career, including a mysterious pair of legs abandoned under a train seat at Waterloo Station in 1935.

Not that the missing leg was going to make much difference to the case anyway, and the head had obviously vanished. What the police, who didn't themselves accept Mahon's story for a minute, wanted most was some means of eliminating the 'reasonable doubt' that a jury might find in his version of the death struggle. This was a very real anxiety on their part at the time, even after all the evidence had been carefully reviewed, and they went ahead with the trial only because there didn't seem any likelihood of the position changing.

This led to J.D. 'Jimmy' Cassels (later Sir James), the former newspaper reporter who had defended Field in the Irene Munro case, being briefed to appear for Mahon. Mr Cassels saw his client at Brixton Prison on several occasions, and on one of them he was told a story which had a most unnerving sequel.

On the Tuesday after escorting Miss Duncan back to London, said Mahon, his return to the bungalow had been made under a stormy sky. As his intention was to destroy the severed head, he built a fierce fire in one of the grates. Then, when the fire was at its hottest, he placed the head upright on the coals. The fair hair lifted in the updraught and burst into flame. And the heat opened those dead eyes to stare at him, just as there was a tremendous thunderclap overhead, followed immediately by lightning that filled the room. This was too much for Mahon: he fled in terror, out into the rain and away across the Crumbles. When he eventually summoned enough courage to return, about three hours later, the head had turned to a skull of ash.

Mr Cassels repeated this tale with caution but, in the event, suffered no embarrassment for having believed it. He also worked very hard and long on his strategy, which included finding an appropriate quotation from William Congreve:

> *Heav'n has no rage, like love to hatred turn'd,*
> *Nor Hell a fury, like a woman scorn'd*

While Mahon prepared himself with confidence for his appearance on Tuesday, July 15, in the County Hall at Lewes, a sleepy little town that came to life only when the Assizes were held.

As has been already remarked, he had a large wardrobe of expensive clothes – they were his chief extravagance – but he still felt the need for a brand-new suit costing nine guineas. The prison pallor of his face troubled him, particularly as a healthy tan had now become the vogue, and he asked for some artificial tanning agent to be bought. This request went unheeded, and so he did what he could with some tobacco juice.

'The bronzed hue of his fine features,' wrote a reporter on the opening day of the trial, 'was a tribute to the extent to which prisoners are now allowed open-air exercise.'

Others went further in their observations, noting that Mahon's delicate hands were curiously white, and that he'd put on weight since the police court hearing.

An American judge sitting beside Mr Justice Avory also caused some interest, as did the exhibits arrayed before the prosecution: a tenon saw, a cook's knife, a flimsy coal scuttle, and a scale model of the bungalow.

For those who had attended the trial of Field and Gray in the same courtroom, it seemed Marshall-Hall's remark about the Crumbles had indeed been prophetic; not only was Mr Justice Avory there, and Mr Cassels, but Sir Henry Curtis-Bennett was again leading for the Crown.

This imposing, portly and brilliant man, with a passion for motor cars, had, in fact, nearly been briefed to represent the accused. He much preferred defending to prosecuting, and had by then fought the death sentence on behalf of more than fifty defendants – taking his failures to achieve an acquittal very hard. 'We are men of the world,' he would often say to a jury; a clever ploy, but they'd know he meant it. His obvious empathy was directed not only at the virtuous either; he became very angry when the Bywaters-Thompson love affair was labelled 'tawdry', and his fondness for Major Herbert Rouse Armstrong, the poisoner, was no secret, however sinister he found him.

But Mahon had an unprecedented effect upon Curtis-Bennett, who said that, after taking one look at him in court, he'd never disliked a prisoner as much. And when Mahon later inspected the grim relics of his crime with the alert interest of an Alsatian being shown a chewed slipper, this dislike was to turn to loathing. Well disguised, of course, but formidable.

The trial began twice. This was again a matter of history repeating itself, because the illness of a juror had halted the proceedings while Gray and Field were in the dock. At the start of the second day a juror fainted, recovered to hear a little more of the evidence about Miss Kaye's past, and suffered another collapse. Then, just as a fresh juror was about to be sworn in, another of the original twelve was taken ill. A second substitute was found and the jury were finally resworn – after a delay which had also lasted five hours.

Nonetheless, despite the fact Curtis-Bennett had to restate his case for the Crown, twenty-eight witnesses gave their evidence before the overnight adjournment.

Third on the list was Chief Inspector Savage. He said that two minute spots of blood had been found on the cauldron, and it was handed to the jury for examination. The cauldron was light and so unsubstantial that the bottom had worn out once already. Its legs were thin and hollow, and one of them was bent.

The chief inspector hadn't been able to find a mark on the door to show where, according to Mahon's statement, the axe had hit it.

But he agreed with Mr Cassels that the accused had volunteered a great deal of information, most of which had proved to be correct. The knife had, for example, been bought at a shop called Staines.

Mrs Elizabeth Bealby Harrison said she was Miss Kaye's sister, and identified a number of her belongings. She spoke about the letters she'd received.

'My sister was very athletic,' Mrs Harrison said. 'I just knew what my sister told me about the man she said she was engaged to (that he was taking her to South Africa), nothing more than I have already said. My sister told me nothing more.'

The judge asked after the deceased's temperament.

'Quiet and rather placid. She did not get into a temper.'

All of her evidence had a strangely flat, noncommital sound to it.

She was followed into the witness box by Miss Ada Constance Smith, the club secretary, who could add little to the picture of the dead woman. 'She told me she was engaged to a man whose name I took to be "Peterson". I knew the name of "Pat"; some man having given me that name on the telephone who wanted to speak to Miss Kaye.'

Miss Edith Mary Warren, a Green Cross Club resident known as 'Phiz', wanted to set the record straight.

'I gave evidence at the police court,' she said, '[but I] did not say there that Miss Kaye was well above the average height of a woman and was physically strong, or anything like it. I said she was shorter than I am, and I said I was 5 ft.

9 in., which is not exceptional.'

Miss Warren had met Mahon at the club, and knew he was the manager of a soda-fountain company. She'd also been shown a diamond and sapphire engagement ring on 'Peter's' return from Bournemouth.

'She asked me to call her Pat by another name because one of the girls at the club knew some business acquaintances of Pat, so she asked me to call him in front of the girls at the club "Derek Patterson".'

If this seemed innocuous enough, the next witness was to produce a very nasty surprise, which incorporated one of those shattering coincidences and a damning lie on Mahon's part.

Mr George Bell Muir began with the evidence expected of him: he explained how he'd acted as an agent for a friend in letting the bungalow, and described arranging the let with a man who called himself 'Waller'.

Then came the crunch. Mr Muir also stated that on April 12, the Saturday Mahon had gone down to live with Miss Kaye at the bungalow, he'd bumped into 'Mr Waller' in Victoria Street, London. And he had noticed that Mr Waller was carrying a bag.

A bag containing a tenon saw, cook's knife and a knife cleaner, according to the evidence of Mr Frederick Charles Stoner, of the Staines Kitchen Equipment Company in Victoria Street. He dithered over the knife cleaner, but had no doubt about selling the prisoner the two other items at around one p.m. Mr Stoner had an invoice carton to prove it.

So Mahon had this equipment before the 'accident', and he hadn't bought it, as his statement claimed, the following Thursday.

Jewellers, chambermaids, hotel receptionists and taxi drivers then did their best to recall – often very vaguely – the movements and purchases of 'Mr and Mrs P. H. Mahon', 'Miss Kaye' and 'Mr J. Waller'.

The second day of the trial ended with two pieces of testimony which were remarkable for their whimsy.

Mrs Florence Amy Gertrude Tate, of 6 Langney Bungalows, described how she had watched the couple walking arm in arm towards the sea.

And a butcher, Mr Frank Francis, told the court of the

difficulty he'd experienced in having them open up and take delivery of some parcels of meat.

The first witness on that heavy, sultry Thursday morning was Mr Reginald Day Finch Hill, who supplied dry details of Miss Kaye's employment as an assistant to Mr Hobbins. She had plainly made no impression on the firm worth mentioning. She had come and she had gone. That was all.

His evidence did, however, contain one piece of information that was worth revealing.

Mrs Mahon was still employed by Consols Automatic Aerators, he said. Most people were pleased to hear that the deception over Mahon's record had not cost her the job she valued so highly.

Even Mahon himself appeared to nod approval. He was as calm and confident as ever, and listened to two more witnesses, both in the hotel trade, without batting an eyelid. They were, after all, saying nothing about his movements he hadn't told the police already.

Then the second of three very imprudent lies caught up with him. This was held to have been the one which made the greatest impression on the jury, although, in actual substance, it lacked the direct relevance of the third.

Miss Ethel Primrose Duncan, who was described as a 'tall, well-built, dark woman', nervously took the oath.

'Do you know the prisoner?' asked Sir Henry.

'Please,' she begged softly, 'do not ask me too many questions.'

'Do you know a man of the name of Patrick Mahon?'

'I do.'

'When did you first meet him?'

'On the tenth of April.'

'Do you remember where?'

'In Richmond.'

Mahon had said in his informal statement that this chance encounter had occurred six weeks before Miss Kaye's death, the jury recalled – not a mere five days. It also meant he had been sniffing about the streets on the eve of his trip to the Crumbles to pick up the keys.

Miss Duncan had been told that his marriage was a 'tragedy' (how true) and that his name was Pat. This had been enough for her to give him her address in Isleworth – or so she implied. Some form of strong attraction must have also played its part.

At this point, Mr Justice Avory interrupted to say: 'I do not gather that the witness has identified the prisoner. You have seen the prisoner, have you not?'

'No, I haven't in court.'

'Let him stand up,' ordered the judge.

'Oh, please don't!'

Miss Duncan broke down as Mahon rose, and there was a short interval before she could carry on again.

'When you gave him your address,' asked Curtis-Bennett, 'did he say anything to you?'

'Asked me if I would dine with him the following week,' answered Miss Duncan, adding that Mahon had made a tentative date for the Wednesday night.

On the Tuesday Miss Kaye met her death, a telegram had arrived from Mahon late in the afternoon: 'Charing Cross 7 tomorrow sure Pat.'

They had dined on Wednesday night at Victoria Station, where Mahon had invited her down to Eastbourne for the Easter weekend. He'd said he was staying there in a friend's bungalow – 'rather a charming place'.

Next day Miss Duncan had received £4 telegraphed to her from Eastbourne, and had used some of it to catch a train down there on Good Friday. After being met at the station, she had lunched and dined in the resort town, before going to the bungalow at about ten in a taxi. There Miss Duncan had spent the night in the bedroom adjoining the one containing the trunk. The court took it for granted that Mahon had shared the same bed.

Miss Duncan had been left in Eastbourne on Easter Saturday while Mahon went to the Plumpton races. They had met up again at the end of the day, dined in an hotel, and had gone back to the bungalow.

On Easter Sunday Mahon had cut his finger on the screw of a lock he was trying to fit to the adjoining bedroom – he had told her that valuable books were stored in there.

'Whilst the prisoner was doing something to the lock, did you see into that room – just a glance?'

'Yes,' sighed Miss Duncan.

'Did you notice anything particular in the room?'

'Yes, I did see the trunk; I was not struck by anything; I

35

saw a trunk and a bed, but it did not interest me at all.'

Later on Mahon had said to her: 'I have locked it up.'

Something which, according to his statements, he'd done before leaving the bungalow to meet her at the station.

Mahon had received a telegram that Sunday, signed by someone called 'Lees' and summoning him to a business meeting. This was to cut short her visit by a day, and Mahon had taken her back to London on Easter Monday, where, after spending the evening together, they had parted at midnight.

'Did the prisoner make any remark to you as to the work that you did in the bungalow?' Sir Henry wanted to know.

'I do not remember now. I think he said he wished – he did not want me to clean to the extent I did.'

'Did he say anything else about it; why he did not want you to do so?'

'Because his wife was coming down the following week, and he did not know what she would say, because – '

Miss Duncan broke down again.

'I'm sorry; she had been down the previous week.'

Mr Cassels began his cross-examination by telling her: 'I do not want to distress you, I only want to ask you one or two questions.'

The first dozen of these were clearly intended to confirm that Mahon's approach to Miss Duncan had been prompted by chivalry. They resulted instead in a fragmentary account so baffling that the jury were left to ponder the strangeness of human nature.

Miss Duncan said that she'd been walking the considerable distance from Kensington to Isleworth when Mahon had spoken to her near a bridge in Richmond. She was very wet at the time.

'Did he offer you a share of his umbrella?' asked Mr Cassels.

'He offered to drive me home.'

'At any rate, did you have the shelter of his umbrella?'

'No.'

'Had he got one?'

'No,' said Miss Duncan.

'Did you tell him you were . . . ?'

The unspoken words brought a deep hush.

'I told him some untruths, I admit.'

An admission that could have been made by Miss Kaye, and one which by now seemed characteristic of the world of Patrick Herbert Mahon. A world of unreality ad-libbed to suit the desires of the weak and pathetic creatures who lived in it – and who could so easily be manipulated by the strong. By predators like Mahon, whose own fantasies were the more convincing – both to themselves and to others – because of being perversions of what they recognized to be the truth.

And this blurring was what had so troubled the police: would the jury be able to tell where the dividing line lay – beyond any reasonable doubt? The trial, however, was now giving everyone present something to *feel*, as well as to see and hear.

Many winced when they heard how close Miss Duncan had come to escaping her nightmare that rainy night.

'I said: "I am sorry, because I do not do things like this," and he said: "Well, it is a tragedy, we will both go our own way." '

But just why she had gone on walking home with Mahon after this exchange wasn't explained; she was probably still searching in herself for the reason.

Before Miss Duncan stepped down, Mr Cassels ended a question with: 'That means you saw no sign of blood about the place?'

'None whatever,' whispered the woman whose body Mahon had also touched on Good Friday.

A refuse collector told the court how he had pointed out where he'd dumped ashes collected at the 'Officer's House'. Bankers gave details of Miss Kaye's transactions, and a stockbroker recalled selling shares on her behalf during February and early April. A ledger keeper said that Mahon's account at Barclay's Bank, Richmond, stood at £40.

All this could have appeared rather dull stuff to the sensation-seekers in the public gallery. Yet several snippets yielded dividends after a moment's reflection. That bank account, for example, was barely a year old, and it wasn't a joint account. From this one might assume that Mrs Mahon had kept control of her share of their double income – if, indeed, she hadn't done more than that, and had kept Mahon fairly short so he couldn't start gambling . . .

Then Mr John Webster, Home Office Analyst, began to

formally identify one blood-stained exhibit after another.

Exhibit 87 was a section of carpet which had been scrubbed clean – but Exhibit 86, a corresponding piece of under-felt, had a large stain soaked into it, and even the floorboards below this had been discoloured. The very act of cleaning the carpet had assisted in the spread of this stain, Mr Webster said, because of the additional moisture.

His evidence should have formed an introduction to the Crown's star witness and the climax of its case, but before Sir Bernard Spilsbury could be called, Mr Cassels begged leave to have Miss Duncan return to the box. It was clear that something important to the defence case had just reached his ear.

Miss Duncan's further ordeal, made worse by the intimacy it implied, did not cause much of a delay. She had remembered seeing four bruises, set close together, on one or other of Mahon's shoulders.

Hindsight would suggest that the defence then erred unwittingly in asking her to point out their approximate position; the bruising did, after all, go some way towards supporting the claim that Mahon had been struck by an axe.

'Where your fingers are?' Mr Cassels asked.

'Just about *there*,' Miss Duncan replied, touching her own shoulder.

Which could possibly have prompted the jury to suppose that the pattern of marks might well have been made by four fingertips.

A recent bruise on the back was given some attention in the early part of Sir Bernard's testimony as an expert witness.

He stood tall and elegant in the box, as immaculate as the rotund fellow-knight examining him, and there was, as always, a red carnation in the lapel of his morning coat.

'The Handsomest Man in London', in the opinion of one newspaper, spoke with simplicity and detachment about the handiwork of the prisoner, a man who regarded himself among the most handsome in the world.

'The breast bone was attached to this piece, and the portions of most of the left ribs.'

'Was the right breast on that piece?' inquired Sir Henry.

'Yes, it was.'

'Is there anything you want to tell us about that?'

'When I pressed it milky fluid escaped from the nipple.'

'You had better say at once,' the judge broke in, 'what that indicates.'

'May I deal with the other piece first, my lord?' said Spilsbury.

'Yes.'

'The fourth piece formed the left side of the chest and on the back of this piece I found an area two inches long over the shoulder-blade which had a recent bruise.'

Sir Henry returned to this injury shortly afterwards: 'Are you able to say at all, from your examination of that bruise, whether it was inflicted shortly before death?'

'Yes, it was certainly inflicted before death. It might have been only a few minutes before death – if it was a very serious blow which had been struck. Or it might have been inflicted a few hours before death, if it had been of a less serious character.'

There had been no sign of any skull or neck bones whatsoever.

'Can you tell us what your opinion is after your examination?'

'As to what?' Mr Justice Avory interjected.

'As to first of all,' Curtis-Bennett explained, 'was this the body of a woman, what size woman, and so on.'

Spilsbury began his methodical but fluent summary, which was to have something of a twist ending:

'All the material I have examined, portions of the trunk, the organs, pieces of boiled flesh, and those fragments of bone which I have been able to identify, are all of them human, and correspond with parts of a single body – no duplicates at all.

'The four pieces of chest and abdominal wall fit accurately to form one trunk, and the organs in the tin box, together with the fragments of organs attached to the four pieces of trunk, form a complete set of human organs – with the exception of certain missing portions, of which the uterus and one ovary are the most important.'

That answered the first question.

'The body was that of an adult female of big build and fair hair.'

That the second; now for what could be deduced.

'She was pregnant, in my opinion, at the time of her death, and at an early period, probably between one and three months. (So, in fact, two lives *had* gone into the balance against those of Mrs Mahon and her daughter.)

'There was no indication of any previous pregnancy, or of pregnancy which had run its full term. The organs were those of a healthy person, and the adhesions round the right lung were the only indication of previous disease.'

Then came the 'catch' conclusion.

'No disease was found to account for natural death – and no condition which would account for unnatural death.'

'I do not follow what that means,' said the judge.

'The head and neck being missing, there was no evidence of the cause of death being some unnatural cause.'

Now the pathologist's careful insinuation was obvious: he couldn't give an opinion about something that wasn't there, so perhaps this was the very reason it wasn't there. Irene Munro's battered skull had allowed for no persuasive stories about an accidental fall. Or, very simply: no head, no evidence – either way.

Mr Justice Avory's response was a striking reminder to every layman of the law's precise use of language, particularly after such a catalogue of hacked-about human tissue.

'In other words,' he said to Spilsbury, 'you found *no evidence of violence* – except the bruise on the back?'

'Except the bruise,' concurred Sir Bernard.

The Crown's case was almost complete. The head had been shown to hold the key to what had really happened, and Curtis-Bennett focused the jury's attention upon it.

'You have seen the coal cauldron, Exhibit 15, which has been produced?' he said to Spilsbury.

'Yes.'

'You have heard, have you not, the statements of the prisoner which have been read?'

'Yes.'

'In your opinion, could Miss Kaye have received *rapidly* fatal injuries from falling on that coal cauldron?'

The stress placed on that word wasn't lost on Mahon – or so it would seem presently – and he looked across intently to hear the reply.

'No, in my opinion, she could not.'

*

More than one eminent barrister had said that Spilsbury was an ideal but deadly witness. There was considerable sympathy for Mr Cassels when he stood up to challenge the expert's views under cross-examination.

'You told us that you found a clean cut of one of the organs, the uterus?'

'Yes.'

'I suppose you found other cuts which were clean, of the internal organs; so far as there were any cuts at all, were they all clean cuts?'

'All except possibly one, they were nearly all clean cuts.'

A small victory for Mr Cassels; this had at least removed any undue significance as to how the uterus – a potent symbol of guilt – had been removed. It could well have become lost, or destroyed with other less emotive organs.

He made this his next point, and Spilsbury confirmed that parts of the stomach, a small gland, and possibly a portion of the intestines were unaccounted for.

But from there on, the defence was checked at every turn.

Brain injuries and compression of the spinal cord were suggested as reasons for Miss Kaye's demise – these failed, because of the circumstances described by Mahon, to secure a satisfactory answer.

'Then there is fracture of the bones of the skull,' said Mr Cassels. 'Does that produce rapid death?'

'Very occasionally; it is not usually rapidly fatal, but certainly fatal in many cases.'

Mr Cassels put that one question too many: 'When you say "not rapidly fatal", do you mean not fatal within an hour?'

Mahon could have sat stunned in the garden for two, three, even four hours, nobody could disprove that.

'Yes, usually not within 24 or 48 hours,' said Spilsbury.

Status lymphaticus was the defence's next hope, and a definition of it was requested.

'That is a condition in which there is a liability to sudden death owing to certain changes in the organs. There may be no violence at all, or it might be very slight violence.' (Status lymphaticus, once an explanation for any seemingly inexplicable death, is today the subject of much controversy; one thing is agreed, however, it can never be a *cause* of death.)

But that idea was totally rejected.

Stabbing, strangulation, throat-slitting . . . and back to the original and most reasonable of suggestions. Miss Kaye had fallen under Mahon's weight and had suffered a mortal head wound when she landed on the cauldron.

'Why not?' Mr Cassels demanded.

'Because no fall on the coal cauldron, such as you have described, would be capable of inflicting such injuries to the head as to cause rapidly fatal results,' said Spilsbury. 'If that particular cauldron, filled with coal, were the one referred to, a sufficiently severe blow to produce such an injury would have crumpled up the cauldron.'

This left the hypothesis of Miss Kaye's neck having been twisted slightly – which could be rapidly fatal in someone with a spinal disease, such as tuberculosis.

'I suppose,' Mr Cassels said finally, 'we need not go so far as to say that *only* diseased persons die from compression of the spinal cord?'

First came the good news.

'Oh, no,' Sir Bernard agreed wholeheartedly.

Then he added: 'It requires extreme violence.'

The jury's verdict now seemed inevitable to many. Mahon had begun his affair with Miss Kaye with a clandestine meeting at a place called Staines, and he had ended it, to all intents and purposes, with a purchase made at a kitchen equipment shop also called Staines. The grim brackets of coincidence . . .

But the man had still to be allowed his own say, and nobody would have wished the trial to end until he'd done so. There was an intense interest in how he would react in the witness box (if ever a monster should be made to squirm it was he, the whispers went), and in the prospect of experiencing something of his personality at first hand (some people being very partial to an attack of the goose pimples). It also had to be conceded that, somehow or other, he might yet be able to induce enough doubt in the jury's mind to escape the hangman.

Mahon, it is said, never doubted this at the outset.

The Crown's case had ended most satisfactorily, from his point of view, with an additional statement he'd made being read out by the Clerk of Assize. This document had begun: 'I have already made a full statement of the facts in this case, but I wish to add some details which may save waste of time and money in calling unnecessary witnesses.' Although these details were little more than a timetable of events, there was an undeniable magnanimity in their provision. Pat, they declared, is an extremely considerate fellow.

And when he took the oath, jaunty in his plum-coloured suit, with its mauve kerchief in the breast pocket, his pleasant, level voice indicated a surprising degree of quiet confidence. A poise which, in fact, looked impossible to shake.

Not that Mahon needed to fear any question put to him that hot afternoon because Mr Cassels was, whether he liked it or not, duty-bound to present his case in the best possible light. Nor could any man have expected him to foresee the shattering phenomenon that Fate had in store.

The prisoner said he was 34 and a married man. A status he had often impressed on Miss Kaye.

His replies were, for the most part, succinct and clearly stated, except for when his gift of the gab got the better of him. The judge said more than once: 'You are asked what you did, not all this imagination.' Mahon took little notice of this – his life depended on the jury's imagination.

He and Miss Kaye had often conversed in French, he said. Her prententiousness – and his own – were transparent in an answer he gave to a question concerning Miss Kaye's job at the Bond Street financier's.

'Miss Kaye was employed as – I suppose an amanuensis is the real term, that is what she described it as.'

An amanuensis, according to *Cassells New English Dictionary*, is: 'A person employed to write what another dictates; a secretary.' And a Latin word, too.

Name-dropping came into his next reply.

'When was it?' asked Mr Cassels.

'Before Christmas, 1923,' said Mahon, ready with his translation. 'She was temporary secretary, and she had inside information from, I think, Colonel Mayes and also, I think it is, Sir William Crossfield, I am not sure.'

Inside information concerning the exchange rate of the franc. Mahon was questioned at length about this joint speculation, towards which he'd allegedly contributed £125 before Christmas. He had been handed the first of the three £100 notes in February, and had cashed it under a false name.

'I was not altogether satisfied about the transaction,' he said, adding for the judge's benefit: 'I mean this: at this period Miss Kaye had not only shown and expressed her love and desire for me, she was not only jealous of my wife, but she was endeavouring, as I thought, to drive a wedge between us, and I wondered if this was part of a plan which I could not see . . . I signed a false name simply so that the note could not be traced back to me.'

Mahon had recovered his capital and had made a small profit. The last of the £100 notes had been given to him on the day before Miss Kaye died.

Mr Cassels then had him recall Miss Kaye's repeated efforts to win him over, and his stubborn refusal to leave his wife. This part of his evidence had that old convincing ring of truth to it – even when he said Miss Kaye must have bought the engagement ring for herself. The two-month let of the bungalow was, however, a puzzling factor.

Taking the bull by the horns, Mr Cassels invited the use of an equally unfortunate expression (even for 1924) when he asked Mahon to state his reason for this.

'. . . it would kill two birds with one stone, if I took the bungalow for that period, and after Miss Kaye had finished down there, and we returned – '

'After Miss Kaye had *finished*?' Mr Justice Avory echoed.

'After we had finished our love experiment, and she returned and I returned, my wife and I could use the bungalow.'

Not a very comfortable sentence.

But Mahon dealt smoothly with the purchases made at Staines Kitchen Equipment Company. He had intended buying a Yale lock to fit to the bungalow's front door – the key he'd been given was too cumbersome – and then had been told by an assistant that the shop was closing. This had happened on the pavement outside, and Mahon had made two impulse-buys from a tray of bargain offers: a knife and a saw, which might turn out to be useful at the Crumbles.

The reconstruction of that fateful evening began.

While Miss Kaye had been writing her letters on their return from London, Mahon had made a fire and heated some milk for them. He had used the axe to break up large lumps of coal.

'I laid the axe carelessly down,' said Mahon, choosing his adverb rather too carefully.

'Tell us where?'

'On one of the tables in the sitting-room.'

There was the row over the letters, and then Mahon had announced he was going to bed. He'd reached the door when Miss Kaye flung the axe at him.

'I was astounded by the suddenness, by the attack altogether, and in a second Miss Kaye followed up the throw. She leaped across the room, clutching at my face – '

Mahon broke down. He didn't touch the neatly-folded mauve kerchief, but dragged a linen square from his trouser pocket and wiped the tears from his eyes.

'We have got as far as she was clutching at your face,' said Mr Justice Avory.

They had fallen after a struggle and Mahon had lost consciousness: 'I think I must have fainted with the fear and with the shock. I do not remember when I did become conscious of what was happening or had happened.'

After dashing water into her face, and having elicited no response, he'd stumbled 'crazy' with fear and fright into the night. He had returned to find her still lying there.

'Can you give us any idea as to what time it would be then?'

'It would be *hours* later, I think; it would be either towards day-break or day-break.'

Mahon recovered his composure with little obvious effort and went on earnestly answering the questions put to him by both his counsel and, less to his liking, the judge. At times he veered too close to the dramatic, but became more sure of himself the longer he spoke.

All sorts of loose ends were tied up. The letter to the club room-mate had been posted posthumously to give him time to think – he'd realized what a fool he had been in not summoning help immediately. Keeping his dinner date with Miss Duncan had been 'a definite thing in my mind to do' amid the confusion, and he had brought her down for 'human companionship' – they'd shared Miss Kaye's vacated bed. The telegram cutting short the weekend he'd sent himself.

Mr Justice Avory balked at the idea of going through the details of the disposal of the body again.

Mahon stood relaxed, waiting his turn to speak quite calmly, while Mr Cassels attempted to justify this line of questioning. The courtroom was stuffy and the late afternoon sunlight very dim. Mr Cassels won his argument.

He turned back to Mahon and said: 'On Tuesday you burned the head – and some portions of the body?'

A deafening clap of thunder shook the building, coming so unexpectedly that it made everyone start. In the flash of lightning which followed, Mahon was seen gripping the edge of the witness box and cowering back, his eyes wide with fright and his face a most perplexing off-white.

The court adjourned a few minutes later; Mr Cassels's quick stream of questions having received, in most cases, a faint 'yes'.

Next morning Mahon looked again a picture of health, and he cocked his head attentively when Sir Henry Curtis-Bennett began the cross-examination. By the end of it, he was not a pretty sight.

The first questions allowed him to repeat answers he'd given several times already, and to his own counsel's apparent satisfaction. Gradually his attitude became less tense as much familiar ground was covered.

The alleged speculation in francs took up some time, without establishing anything other than Mahon's lack of information about it: an ignorance based on trust.

His illicit relationships with both Miss Kaye and Miss Duncan were also examined at length, and Mahon explained them in terms of his lamp-post philosophy, often appearing surprised that some points weren't patently obvious. His continued allegiance to Mrs Mahon being one of them; he clearly felt he belonged to her, whatever he might do when roaming abroad on his own, and would always return to her side.

The thickets of his deceits were explored. Mahon had used some enormously complicated ruses to keep potentially troublesome people like Mr Muir at bay. Several of his plans, such as the one for retrieving a letter sent to an imaginary referee in the Midlands, were really quite ingenious, and he outlined them with due modesty.

'Pure invention?' Sir Henry suggested.

'Pure invention,' Mahon affirmed.

And found himself suddenly in the open, twisting from one side to another to fend off attack.

'When did you remember that you had bought that knife

and saw on the 12th of April?' asked Sir Henry.

'Not until my statement was read out at Hailsham police court.'

'Did you make up your mind to say that you had bought the knife and saw upon the 12th of April after you had heard evidence which was called at Hailsham police court from the Staines equipment company?'

'I don't quite follow,' said Mahon.

Making him about the only person in the room who didn't: the revised date of purchase was the soft underbelly of his evidence. Sir Henry pursued the point relentlessly.

'There were mistakes regarding the dates,' Mahon said in exasperation.

'I am going to draw your attention to one or two.'

'Mistakes regarding one or two things which could only have been made by someone in mental agony at the time!'

But Mahon had made a number of alterations to the statement in question. Surely the inference had been that he'd bought the tools for the purpose of getting rid of the body.

'It's all so futile, when you come to think of it,' whimpered Mahon, losing control of himself. 'This is the position: the knife and saw were bought by me for an innocent object! The name was on the knife. I told them the name of the shop and I told them I bought the saw. It's utterly absurd for a man to try and confuse the dates!'

He was reminded that it had been a cash sale, and so his identity had not been required for the invoice.

'Kenilworth Court Hotel, Eastbourne, Monday: "Dear Old Fizzy" – you knew who that was, did you?'

'I never heard Miss Warren called "Phiz".'

That was a feint – and Sir Henry would return to 'Phiz' with devastating effect. He asked Mahon to define the expression 'seeing red'.

'One gets angry.'

'Would it be right to say you saw red during this struggle with Miss Kaye?'

'I saw many things besides red.'

'I dare say.'

Back to the knife again. Mahon was asked why he had used the carving knife provided by his landlord, and not the new knife, for cutting up his lover's body.

The day before Mahon had told Mr Cassels that he'd worn

a sling because his wrist had been injured in preventing an old lady from falling off a bus. If that had been the sort of thing which made Mr Justice Darling wince, then the prisoner was about to go one better.

'For the reasons perhaps you know, Sir Henry,' replied Mahon.

'I should like to hear it.'

'It is this,' he said, pointing to the carving knife, 'Miss Kaye had used with me the other knife, the chef's knife, the cook's knife, and I picked *that* knife.'

In short: for sentimental reasons.

But Mahon wasn't as confident as he'd sounded then: he was shivering. Soon he would again protest the futility of trying to give an honest answer to the Crown's questions – he even complained to the judge about the 'unfair' tactics being used on him. His whines went ignored.

Sir Henry pointed out that the words 'she was in trouble' had been deleted from the first statement made at Scotland Yard. Aggrieved to find this counted as evidence, Mahon offered an involved explanation.

'You did use the expression "she was in trouble",' Sir Henry summed up for him, 'but you meant she was in trouble with someone at the club?'

'That is what I meant.'

'You've heard Sir Bernard Spilsbury's evidence?'

'Yes.'

'That at the mouth of the uterus there was a clean cut and that the uterus itself is missing?'

'Yes.'

'Is that pure coincidence?'

'Pure coincidence,' said Mahon, who'd already sworn he wouldn't know a uterus if he saw one.

And probably it was: *none* of that body was meant to have been discovered.

The missing head came next. Sir Henry tried without success to have him give the time that it had been in the fire.

'Are you not clear about the time? This was a terrible thing you were doing. Did you not realize how long it took?'

Mahon paused before answering.

'If you knew the circumstances in which this head was burned – I can only say burned,' he began, faltered, and went on, 'I could not even stay in the room while it was burning.'

When it was implied that this wasn't what had happened to the head – because no trace of its incineration had been found – Mahon looked hurt.

'Where did you throw the bones of this most important part of the body, the skull?'

'I threw them over the garden wall. They were tremendously small bones.'

They had landed on the shingle.

'What did you break them with?'

'I broke them in my hands like this,' said Mahon, innocent of the effect of his demonstration. 'After they came out of the fire, they would break just like *that*.'

The gesture chilled; and a few seconds later Curtis-Bennett was sickened into a moment's heavy sarcasm.

'I suggest to you that would be impossible.'

'Your suggestion is entirely wrong, Sir Henry.'

'I may have leave to call Sir Bernard about it?'

'That,' growled Mahon, a bone expert in his own right, 'is a thing I know.'

And was caught off-guard as Curtis-Bennett closed for the kill. This time the evidence about Miss 'Phiz' Warren would drive him back, craven and casting desperate looks of appeal at the jury.

The attack was based on the letter which, in Mahon's own words, had precipitated Miss Kaye's assault on his person. The letter she'd tossed across to him and told him to sign 'Pat'. A letter she'd actually begun to sign herself . . .

'It starts "Dear Old Phiz"?'

'I know.'

'Do you really mean that Miss Kaye that night, besides being in this paroxysm of rage, was also in the sort of mood she was writing a letter to a strange *man* beginning "Dear Old Phiz"?'

'It may sound strange to you,' said Mahon, 'but that is what happened.'

Mr Justice Avory asked who the man was.

'I mentioned yesterday he was the assistant secretary of the Richmond bowls tournament of which I was the honorary secretary.'

'Was he ever called by this nickname?' asked the judge.

'No, my lord. I think I commented that it was so absurd to

address him as "Dear Old Phiz", because he is a solemn sort of individual.'

'It was an extraordinary thing for a lady like Miss Kaye to do, was it not?' said Sir Henry, raising his brows.

'Yes, I know.'

'Just let us read what you refused to sign . . .'

And Sir Henry Curtis-Bennett drew particular attention to the first sentence.

Dear Old Phiz,

I am sorry I shall not after all be able to see you before my departure.

You can imagine there has been a lot to do and I have not been able to see quite a lot of people before packing up. We shall be travelling overland through France and Italy en route for the Cape.

On our arrival there I will write to you fully regarding prospects and other matters in general, but I really wish to thank you in this letter for all the kindness and good fellowship you have shown me in the past. One cannot put into words just what one feels, but I am sure if I say just this, that you will understand and appreciate just what is in my mind.

Any letter addressed to me c/o The Standard Bank, Cape Town, will find me, but as I said in an earlier part of my letter, I will write to you fully on my arrival.

With every good wish, believe me,

Yours P

And there it stopped. At *P*.

Cut short by the guile of a woman called Peter.

Or, perhaps, at that very second, by a murderous blow from behind.

The American judge watched the closing stages of the trial with awed solemnity, and then admitted to being utterly astonished by what happened at the end of it.

After commenting on Mahon's behaviour following the dismemberment on the Crumbles, Sir Henry completed his speech for the Crown with these words:

'Nobody noticed anything untoward about him at all, and you may have your opinion as to whether the feeling he showed in the witness box was real or not.'

Mr Cassels quoted William Congreve, and then added his own touch of poetic imagery:

'Can you conceive that, possibly on the threshold of eternity, you would get play-acting from a man in such a grave position?'

The jury slept on it. They had also to consider a piece of additional evidence which had brought Sir Bernard Spilsbury back to the box. There he'd stated emphatically that the carving knife could not have made the clean cuts he had found – whereas the cook's knife, which was designed for dividing raw meat, could have.

On Saturday morning, Mr Justice Avory referred to the choice of three verdicts which Mr Cassels had placed before them: guilty of murder, guilty of manslaughter – or not guilty at all. For Mahon to be found not guilty, the judge cautioned, the jury would have to conclude that he'd had to kill in order to save his own life.

They retired to consider their verdict at 12.7 p.m. They were back in 45 minutes.

The prisoner was to die for the crime of wilful murder.

Mahon's face went that odd colour again; his tobacco-juice tan making visible a mask of sham which so many had, to their cost, failed to see.

Shaking, he gripped the edge of the box.

'I feel too conscious of the bitterness and unfairness of the summing-up which you have uttered,' he told the judge, 'to say anything except I am not guilty of murder.'

The black cap was placed on the judge's wig.

Mr Justice Avory prefaced his dread words by reminding Mahon that, in mercy to him, the jury had not known of his Guildford conviction. And after passing the death sentence, he made these the final words of the trial:

'It may perhaps interest the jury to know that the reference I made to the prisoner's previous history was a conviction for an assault upon a woman . . .'

That this information should be revealed, when all was said and done, was what so astonished the American guest sitting beside him.

On the threshold of eternity, Mahon confessed – but asked that this shouldn't be publicized for fear of the 'bad impression it might make'.

And then he did something equally in character, if paradoxical, which horrified the witnesses to his execution.

Man has the unique capacity to suppress his instincts even in situations where his whole being shrieks out against this. He can be expected to go to his certain death with dignity, knowing that resistance would be pointless, and hoping only that it will be said he died like a man.

Mahon's death had no dignity; he died like a dog.

Everyone entering the execution chamber could see at once that there was no escape from the position chalked on the wide trap.

Tom Pierrepoint worked swiftly; he dropped the hood over the prisoner's head and stepped back to pull the lever. As he did so, Mahon, pinioned hand and foot, made a desperate, instinctive leap forward to save himself somehow. But the trap crashed open beneath him, and he swung back, striking the base of his spine against the scaffold's edge. Then the thread, which held the rope's slack in a coil, snapped – and Mahon plunged out of sight.

'That blow killed him,' said Roland Wild and Derek Curtis-Bennett, in their 1937 biography of Sir Henry, and they further described Mahon as 'doubly hanged'. Which could be interpreted as meaning that Mahon had finally cheated the law by taking the initiative and committing suicide, in a manner of speaking.

The evidence, however, suggests differently. It also provides what some may find a more apposite ending to the story of Patrick Herbert Mahon and the men who hunted him down.

Every execution was followed almost immediately by a post-mortem and a formal inquest in the prison where it had taken place. The one at Wandsworth on September 9, 1924, was the first of fifty or more such inquests for which that most meticulous of men, Sir Bernard Spilsbury, received a small fee.

The customary procedure was for the prison doctor to open the neck and leave it at that. When the coroner saw the body stripped of its suit and being opened right up, he dropped a hint or two, mindful of the jury waiting to hear the inquest. Only his tact was appreciated.

Spilsbury, who performed a thousand autopsies a year, examining each body minutely, even if it had come from under a bus, politely insisted on doing things his way.

He spent an hour on the body, but his case card, headed *Judicial Hanging*, makes no mention of a bruise on the back, self-inflicted or otherwise. Then he spent another hour on Mahon's brain alone, and took away a piece of it in his own black bag.

Chapter Two

THE CASE OF SIDNEY FOX:
MURDER AT THE METROPOLE

REX *v.* SIDNEY HARRY FOX

MARCH, 1930

Sidney Harry Fox cooked his goose the night he set fire to a French newspaper under his mother's armchair. His virtues were few, his vices innumerable, but he did break a pattern.

Almost exactly three months after Mahon's execution, a two-timing poultry farmer, who had kept cuttings of the case, decapitated his fiancée and buried her dismembered body in his chicken run.

At Lewes Assizes, Sir Henry Curtis-Bennett appeared for the Crown, and Mr J. D. Cassels, KC, defended the farmer, whose fate was sealed by Sir Bernard Spilsbury.

And so Mahon's last wish was granted, inasmuch as he left a favourable impression in some quarters at least. While it could also be said that his gift of salesmanship transcended the grave.

On May 5, 1927, an estate agent went out of his way to buy a cook's knife from the Staines Kitchen Equipment Company in Victoria Street, London. He used it to cut up a woman whose body he left in a trunk at Charing Cross Station. Following the phew and cry in the cloakroom, Spilsbury sealed his fate, too.

By now that useful piece of luggage was earning itself an unenviable reputation in the South of England. Soon its repeated use would link it forever with Brighton.

But the rival resort of Margate was, however, first to be the scene of a crime judged more horrible than plain murder. And, by the way of a change from murderers of the more conventional sort, the chief protagonist would be a 31-year-old homosexual nicknamed Cupid.

Or, as his old mum liked to call him, her 'clever Sidney'.

It was nearing midnight at the Metropole, one of the best commercial hotels in Margate, when the travelling salesmen in the lounge and billiard room heard a commotion.

And saw a young gentleman come running down the main staircase in only a vest.

'Where's the boots?' he cried out, in a noticeably genteel accent. 'I believe there's a fire!'

Sam Hopkins tried to find the 'boots', spread the alarm, and then rushed up to Room 67, followed by four or five other commercial travellers. He was shown in, found it full of smoke, and retreated into the passage.

'My mother's in there!' the young gentleman said, pointing to the next door along.

Someone opened it. Here the smoke was like a wall; black, pungent and so dense that Hopkins could see nothing through it – except a faint glimmer to his left. He plunged into the room, but was driven back. He tried again, holding a handkerchief over his nose and mouth, but this didn't help. Then he noticed there was a layer of air about six inches deep over the floor.

Hopkins threw himself flat and, using his elbows, wormed his way blindly forward until his hand touched a cold foot. He staggered up, got a grip under the arms, and pulled the person off the bed.

Backing out into the passage, Hopkins saw that he'd rescued a short, stout old woman, who was wearing nothing but a vest, and whose toothless mouth hung open.

'My mummy, my mummy,' he heard the ineffectual young gentleman sob.

Hopkins covered her nakedness with his raincoat, while calling on the others there to help. Then he dragged the old woman another three yards before collapsing.

That was the last Sam Hopkins remembered of October 23, 1929; the day he had decided to give the Metropole a try – not too pricey but different, they said.

The best account of what happened next was given by Dr Robert William Nichol, the second of two doctors to be summoned by the management. He arrived to find a colleague, Dr Cecil Austin, kneeling beside an old woman covered in coats in the hall. From her colour, she looked ill, but Dr Austin came over to say Mrs Fox was dead. There had been a fire in her bedroom, and she'd died of shock and of being suffocated by the smoke.

The two doctors then went up to Room 66, accompanied by the hotel manager and the police.

It was now midnight.

Although the window had been opened, the air was still foul with smoke so thick and greasy that it had ringed the nostrils of guests merely grabbing a look.

There was a hole burned in the Wilton carpet about a yard from the gas fire, and a quantity of newspaper lay scattered about, some of it in ashes. Dr Nichol noticed the impression of a heavy body on the bed, and a large damp patch of urine on the bedding. The police asked him to examine three bottles; two held a bitter tonic, he told them, and the third contained petrol, used for cleaning clothes. Then an armchair was carried back into the room and placed over the hole in the carpet.

The Margate fire chief, Mr Harry Hammond, took a look at this chair. Only the underneath part had been damaged, and it'd been a smouldering fire, rather than one involving flames. Mr Hammond reasoned that some garment, probably the burned combination, had been hung on the arm to dry. It had caught alight and dropped to the floor – the rest followed logically.

That seemed to take care of the dead. So Dr Nichol concerned himself with the welfare of the living, and went in search of Sidney Fox, whom everyone informed him had been a very devoted son.

Dr Nichol found Fox in the private sitting-room to which he'd been taken while the police were still trying artificial respiration. He was in a chair and the manager's wife was trying to comfort him, by telling him that his mother might not be dead after all, and by stroking his head. Fox did not appear consoled, and Dr Nichol took pains to break the bad news to him in a circumspect way.

Fox was perplexed by the murmured remarks made about an inquest, and about how it was necessary for the coroner to inquire into any and every violent death. Then he realized that his mother must be dead and 'doubled up' – to use Dr Nichol's own phrase. After a while, he asked if he might see her again.

The body had been locked in a top-floor room to await the undertakers. Inspector William Palmer, the coroner's officer, escorted them up there, accompanied by the hotel manager, whose night this wasn't.

Before withdrawing, to allow Fox some privacy, Dr Nichol

saw him walk up to the body very naturally and touch it gently.

Fox kept them only a few moments. On the way downstairs again, Dr Nichol suggested that he should have a legal representative at the inquest, just in case there were any insurance policies involved. This advice was received without comment, but Dr Nichol, who was distressed by Fox's condition, persisted in trying to help him adjust to what had happened. To this end, he followed him into the room which the manager had provided for the rest of the night.

There Fox told him what a good mother she had been. And remarked on what a curious coincidence it was that Walburgar, Lady Paget, had died in much the same fashion only recently, not long after being in touch.

His agitation increased; he began bemoaning the fact he'd retired much earlier than usual, and fretting over £24 which his mother had put in her handbag – wherever that had got to. Dr Nichol made him get into bed and gave him an injection of morphine.

Then Inspector Palmer came in at about 12.20 a.m. and asked if Fox would give him a statement for the inquest.

Fox said his mother's age was 63, and that they were of independent means.

'We have recently been on holiday in France,' he went on, 'where my mother has been visiting the graves of my brothers killed in the war. She was quite well and a healthy woman, and I had never known her to have a day's illness.'

Although, of course, three days before on the Sunday, she had complained of a slight chill, for which Dr Austin had prescribed a mixture.

The previous evening, he had lit his mother's gas fire for her at about 9.45 p.m., and had left her, fully dressed and reading a paper, to go down to the bar. An hour later he had taken himself to bed in the adjoining room, which had a connecting door.

'I was aroused at about 11.30 by what I thought was a window rattling,' said Fox. 'I noticed a smell of fire. I closed my window and went to her room to see if it came from there. I found her room full of smoke; there was a light near where the stove would be.'

Unable to enter the room, he'd rushed downstairs to get help from the porter.

Fox burst into tears twice while giving his statement and had to ask Inspector Palmer for a glass of water. Then, when it was over, he asked:

'Have you found my mother's handbag? – as it contains a lot of money.'

'How much?' said Inspector Palmer.

'There is £24 in notes, I know. I went to London yesterday to change a cheque for Mother for £25 at her bank in London.'

Dr Nichol, who had made another of his discreet withdrawals, then insisted that Fox should get some sleep, and they left him with a promise that a search would be made for the money.

A police constable had the handbag. It was burned on the outside, and had a small scorch the size of a pea on the inside, but they didn't find any cash.

Which didn't unduly surprise the manager of the Hotel Metropole, Mr Joseph Harding, who had been keeping a leery eye on the family Fox. Either they were the genuinely eccentric rich, or one had to jump to an obvious conclusion from the squalid way they lived.

As Mr Harding told his wife, while they were preparing for bed after the last policeman had gone, the search for the money in Room 66 had allowed him to take a good look around.

What he'd seen there had confirmed that: neither guest had any night attire, nor had they a change of clothing or a toothbrush – and the pair of false teeth, lying in Mrs Fox's washbasin, had been disgustingly dirty.

The fact remained, however, whether a swindler or no, and they hadn't any actual proof of dishonesty, young Fox's devotion to his old mother had been beyond question. Her sudden passing had come as a terrible shock to him, as anyone else could see, and even a rogue was entitled to be left alone in his grief.

Then again, rich or poor, straight or crooked, with people like the Foxes, stupid accidents were almost bound to happen.

Mrs Harding was sniffing her hand. It wasn't Fox she smelt, but something else.

'That boy's hair is full of smoke,' she told her husband, 'and he says he never went near the room!'

The Hardings stared at one another. There was an obvious conclusion to be drawn from this as well. But to think that, would be to think the unthinkable – and besides, it didn't make sense.

That same morning, the inquest on Mrs Rosaline Fox, of End View, Lyndhurst, returned a verdict of accidental death; and Room 66 on the third floor of the Metropole fell vacant once more, thanks to a prompt removal by Gore Brothers.

It wasn't as easy to get shot of Sidney. He stayed on until the following day, distributing his mother's effects among the staff, and receiving much sympathy.

'What are you going to do?' asked Miss Gwendoline Bugg, as she served him his lunch after the inquest. 'You will have to get married.'

'I shall probably go to Australia,' he said.

Then Fox found Inspector Palmer waiting to tell him that there was no trace of the £24, and to query the sum again. Fox was adamant: he had drawn £25 from Lloyds bank at 39 Threadneedle Street, taken a pound of it for himself, and given the balance to his mother. They got talking.

Fox explained that he and Mrs Fox had been on their way to a new home at Lyndhurst, having intended to stay in Margate only just for one day, but his mother simply hadn't felt up to travelling. His father, Mr William Fox, dead these sixteen years, poor old chap, had been the proprietor of Fox's Flour Mills at East Dereham, which the inspector had probably heard of. Fox had been educated at Framlingham College, where he'd been a boarder in East House under Rose, an awfully good type. And so on. Just the sort of thing one would expect from a young man of his class being asked a lot of inane questions.

'Your mother had no night attire,' remarked Inspector Palmer.

His impertinence was overlooked, and Fox replied lightly: 'My mother has worn none for some time.'

Mr Harding overheard this conversation.

He also received a telephone call from the Royal Pavilion Hotel in Folkestone. It had likewise enjoyed the patronage of Mrs Fox and her son – until they'd left without paying their bill. Of course, there wasn't anything along these lines in the paper, but nevertheless . . .

By then Fox had paid his bill at the Metropole – after a fashion; he had asked for it to be sent to his new solicitor in the town. Moreover, he had given a forwarding address, and he'd sweetly posted a highbrow book from there to Miss Vera Hopper, the Metropole receptionist, together with a sad little note.

Even so, Mr Harding could no longer contain his worst suspicions, and went to tell the police the embarrassingly far-fetched-sounding story about Mrs Harding's smoky hands. Nobody laughed: he was advised to charge Fox with obtaining food and accommodation by false pretences.

And he did.

On November 3, Inspector Palmer saw Fox at Margate police station. The prisoner had been arrested by Sergeant Fleet, one of the officers who had tried to revive his mother, and who'd caught up with him in Norwich.

Fox was being held on six fraud charges, and these charges were all that they discussed. But a collection of pawn tickets found in his pockets, together with his mother's rings, began to tell something of the true story. Especially when they were listed – for safekeeping – in chronological order:

gold watch, 2s 3d – March 30
diamond ring, £2 – June 3
gold wrist watch, 8s 6d – June 3
leather case, 15s – June 20
pair of trousers, 5s – June 25
safety razor, 1s 3d – July 8
raincoat, 8s 6d – October 7

More immediate was the telegram sent from Margate by an ex-policeman working as an insurance claims investigator:

EXTREMELY MUDDY WATER IN THIS BUSINESS

That made waves. On October 21, the Monday of the week in which Mrs Fox had tragically passed on, her son had been in London to extend insurance cover until midnight on Wednesday. Insurance which, provided she died by accident, would pay out £2,000. Mrs Fox had met every provision, if only by twenty minutes.

Scotland Yard was alerted. For Chief Inspector Hambrook, it was like having news of an old friend: on November 5 the hotel bedroom was revisited, and on November 7 the Yard had arrived officially in Margate to be of assistance.

Inspector Palmer had never heard a word about insurance.

Two days later at noon, Mr Herbert Gore was back in the churchyard at Great Fransham, Norfolk, with an unpaid bill for £47 10s in his pocket, watching a polished oak coffin being raised from its grave. Undertakers cannot repossess their goods, but possibly derive some small inner satisfaction from an exhumation.

Particularly when they have done their work as well as Mr Gore, and can demonstrate as much to an authority like Sir Bernard Spilsbury.

In a nearby schoolroom, Mr Gore broke the seal of putty and lifted the lid, stepping back to allow Sir Bernard his nose. The only odour was that of clean, dry sawdust.

Then the pathologist cast a discerning eye over the contents and saw a remarkably well-preserved old woman, who wore nothing but a short vest, and who was heavy for her size. Her hair was grey and white and scanty, and her aquiline nose had an old scar across the bridge. Her face was broad and high-cheeked, with a wide, loose-lipped mouth.

The sexton was asked if he could formally identify the remains. His appalled eye saw a corpse coloured green, crimson, blue and cheese yellow, but he unhesitatingly stated that it was Old Rosy, whom he'd have known anywhere. In fact, Sexton Arthur Cross, a wheelwright by trade, had known her father, a farm labourer; her husband, a signalman; her lover, a porter; her three eldest sons – and, of course, her favourite, young Sid, about whom many a tale could be told.

Which was exactly what the police had been finding out for themselves, starting with the tales told directly to them.

Sir Bernard's first concern was to look for signs of poisoning, as this seemed the obvious thing to do in a case where there'd been no post-mortem. Then he got on to searching for soot – and for bruises.

A new line of investigation that would lead to Inspector Palmer going that evening, in those days before the National Health Service, to ask a maid at the Hotel Metropole if he could have Mrs Fox's teeth back.

But one which, upon reflection, grew fairly naturally out of what everyone remembered best of that very short inquest.

'Now, tell me, Fox,' the coroner had said kindly, 'what condition was your mother in last night? Was she cheerful?'

'Oh, yes; quite well. Just before she went to bed we had a

61

sham fight – you know, a boxing match.'

'What! *A boxing match?*'

'Only in fun, of course,' Fox had assured him.

Three thousand people had applied for the fifty seats available to the public at Lewes Assizes when Mahon stood in that dock. About as many applied to see Fox appear there on Wednesday, March 12, 1930.

If one has ever wondered why some trials of that era became notorious while others, just as dramatic or horrifying in their own right, passed almost unnoticed, then part of the answer is to be found in the patronage they received. A large proportion of these applicants belonged to the so-called leisured classes – to the 'smart set' whose antics and tastes the popular Press avidly recorded for the edification of the masses. Putting it crudely, they gave a trial snob appeal.

While incurring the wrath of Sir Henry Curtis-Bennett, who described the rows of fashionably-dressed men and women, with their blasé expressions and opera glasses, as that 'senseless and morbid crew'.

He was indeed back at Lewes, now weighing in for the Crown at just under twenty stone, and Mr Cassels was there too, ready to do his damnedest for the defence. A few feet away sat Sir Bernard Spilsbury.

But although the heavens would spring another surprise, making at least some comparison with the Mahon trial unavoidable, the scene owed far more to the poultry farmer's hearing. That was when the amazing Dr Robert Matthew Brontë had flatly contradicted Spilsbury's findings – before spoiling the effect by going on to talk about how a chicken could run about without a head. The former Crown Analyst for All Ireland had since said some sillier things than that, but here he was again, all rarin' to go.

While Fox, in a dark tie and black overcoat, looking altogether very dapper, if noticeably white-skinned, waited – as blasé as anyone behind him – for Mr Justice Rowlatt to appear. Those seeing the prisoner for the first time were struck by his high, domed forehead, his bushy hair and his drooping left eyelid. A disfigurement which gave his otherwise pleasantly-featured face a decided 'good side' and 'bad side', and allowed the more imaginative to suppose some natural law had been at work.

The judge entered and the trial began.

Like most trials, it could reveal only a very small part of the real story – just enough to be fatal – and it would also be extremely misleading at times, however unintentionally. When, for example, Mr Cassels said that Fox had been brought up by his widowed mother, and had 'known no other companion', there must have been hoots of nervous laughter in certain select circles.

Sidney Harry Fox was born under mysterious circumstances in the last year of the 19th century.

All that can be said with any confidence is that he did not share the same sire as the first three Fox brothers. Great Fransham simply assumed that his father had been the railway porter for whom the brazen-faced Rosy had deserted her signalman husband. But Fox seems to have had grounds for believing that he was partly of noble birth, and his mother may well have told him as much, for reasons of her own. Whatever the truth of the matter, this conviction was to dominate his life, and particularly his attitude to work.

He was excellent at writing at school, and did very well at recitation – two gifts he was later to pervert to criminal purposes. He was also passably ingenious, and began his police record at eleven with a plan which must have appeared foolproof in theory.

Fox went collecting for a charity. On each doorstep, he would note down the amount received in his official collecting book, and have the benefactor sign it. Nothing could have seemed more above board, nor any grateful little smile as beguiling. But before he handed his book back to the organizers, Fox glued two pages together and pocketed the difference.

His plan didn't come unstuck exactly. It was just that someone noticed how much thicker one page was than the rest. The meanness of the offence led to the police being notified and, in due course, Fox was birched.

This episode taught him a lesson he never forgot: there was definitely money to be made out of the inherent goodness of others.

In 1914 he and his mother left Great Fransham and moved to London, where Fox's cherubic and trustworthy looks did him proud. He became page boy to Sir John and Lady Constance Leslie of Manchester Square.

Above stairs he was a palpable hit. The doting family called him 'Cupid' and thought it very unjust of the other servants to try and blame him for their own mistakes. In return, Fox behaved with exemplary kindness towards old Sir John, and led him patiently around the square every afternoon.

Fox had learned another lesson – much the same one as Mahon had done: that even sensible people very often preferred to rely on their sight rather than on their hearing.

Below stairs he was loathed. The chief cause of this was the favouritism shown to him, particularly when he passed on the blame for his own mistakes to his fellow servants. But this didn't bother Fox.

Godolphin Horne was Nobly Born;
He held the Human Race in Scorn

There is, in fact, a great deal about this watershed in Fox's career to remind one of the *Cautionary Tales* told in verse by Hilaire Belloc, which dealt almost exclusively with wayward young men who doomed themselves in similar households.

His arrival in Manchester Square had confirmed the aristocratic notions Fox held about himself, and, feeling so very much at home, it wasn't long before he could mimic the speech and manners of the upper class to his satisfaction.

But mimicry has its price, when it comes to wearing the right clothes on one's afternoons off, and Fox stole some of the silver when he was sixteen. Then he fleeced an elderly housemaid of her life savings.

That did it. The family were obliged to listen to the other servants for once, and both of Fox's crimes came to light. He was dismissed instantly, but the Leslies, grateful for Cupid's three years of service, didn't prosecute. There could have been quite a banging about of pots in the kitchen that night, and it's just possible that the soup at dinner was cold.

Mrs Fox, whose third son by Mr Fox had been killed in an explosion at Woolwich Arsenal that year, welcomed Sidney back with open arms. Not long afterwards, her clever son had a good position in a bank. He also had a crack at forgery.

Clemency was again shown to him, only this time there was a catch to it: Fox could either face prosecution – or he could join the army.

He joined the army and became a cadet in the Royal Flying Corps. It is reasonable to suppose that it was at this stage, amid all that masculine hurly-burly, Fox discovered he was an invert – as homosexuals were then known. Perhaps the discovery was made for him by some superior with an eye for a pretty lad, as certain records seem to indicate. But the how and why don't really matter; the important thing is that Fox became intensely proud of his proclivity, and Cupid had added another string to his bow.

But he hadn't forgotten the Leslies of Manchester Square. Fox went down to Brighton one day and introduced himself to an old family friend as Sir John's grandson. His dress was right, his manner was right, and his engaging patter was right – as well as being correct down to the last second cousin, twice removed. His hostess was delighted by this surprise visit, and by the latest snippets of news he had brought with him.

He had also brought a blank cheque book which he'd stolen while distributing the post during a short stay in hospital.

Eventually Fox asked if there was any way in which he could cash a cheque, as he had been idiotic enough to run a trifle short. Of course, there was. She sent a maid with him down to her greengrocer, and a cheque for £5 was cashed on the spot.

To the dismay of the greengrocer, the cheque was returned marked 'no account' and he had to explain this to her ladyship. The real grandson then made it indignantly clear that a fraud had been perpetrated.

Nothing much happened.

Mrs Fox's second son by Mr Fox was killed in action, and she was awarded a pension of 10s a week for his sacrifice.

Fox continued to enjoy life at what some might term its best: he dined at the finest clubs, drank champagne in dressing-rooms, and indulged himself sexually without fear of conception.

Then, as 1917 drew to a close, the gods pulled one of their dirtier tricks by sending Captain Glynes Bruty down to Brighton for a few days' holiday at Christmas.

A can of worms was about to lose its lid.

Captain Bruty was an Assistant Provost Marshal of the East-

'ern Command (a senior officer in the military police), and a man who couldn't take a real holiday if he tried.

Inevitably, he ended up talking shop with the Brighton police, and heard about a greengrocer who had been defrauded. There was a suspect of sorts, he was told, to wit: a former page boy at Manchester Square called Fox. But while Fox might have all the inside information necessary for such a daring swindle, it seemed hardly likely that he could have impersonated a gentleman so successfully.

Captain Bruty went back to London and made some inquiries at Manchester Square and the bank, probably having reasons of his own for being interested in Fox. These inquiries resulted in a plain-clothes military policeman calling on the cadet's mother.

Lieutenant Fox wasn't at home, Mrs Fox apologized. There were all sorts of places he might be, such as at the Royal Automobile Club, of which he was a member.

Nonsense, said the club secretary. No 'Lieutenant Fox' appeared on their list. But Captain Bruty checked further and discovered that mail arrived there addressed to 'The Honourable S. H. Fox' – there was, as it happened, just such a letter on the rack at the time. The hall porter remembered it being left by an elderly officer.

Captain Bruty ignored the scribbled injunction to 'Await arrival' and opened the envelope. Inside was a most damning piece of evidence: a letter of considerably more than endearment written on the notepaper of a famous club. There was no name to it, simply two initials.

The envelope was resealed and replaced in the rack. Captain Bruty and a plain-clothes man then took up inconspicuous positions on either side of it, and began a wait which ended at seven-thirty that evening.

Fox sauntered up to the letter rack, read his note, and tore it into pieces, which he dropped in a waste-paper basket. Then he sat down outside the waiting room.

The plain-clothes man made a dive for the waste-paper basket, while Captain Bruty confronted Fox and asked him about his courtesy title, his membership of the club, and his commission in the army.

'I got a chit to say I was going to be gazetted, when I was in hospital,' he explained airily.

'That does not make you an officer,' replied Captain Bruty,

showing his hand by adding: 'and you are not an officer. You must come with me.'

At military police headquarters, Fox was ordered to turn out his pockets.

The cheque book used at Brighton was only one of half a dozen he had on him. He was also carrying sheets of blank notepaper, filched for their letterheads from the writing rooms of various hotels and clubs, and a wad of salacious correspondence. But most unbecoming an officer and a gentleman was the rouge and other face make-up.

The initialled letter, now carefully pasted together on a piece of tissue paper, was added to the collection.

And Fox blurted out the name.

The writer of the note was cashiered, and became effectively the first person Fox is known to have destroyed. This was, however, something of an accident, whereas the next time he would attempt murder.

The military police handed him over to the civilian authorities and he served three months' hard labour, some of which involved army training. His exertions in this respect were found to have aggravated an epileptic tendency in him – whatever that means – and he was later granted a life pension of 8s a week.

The 90-day stretch doesn't appear to have done Fox much harm otherwise. He remained a particular favourite with certain officers until peace came, and then took more to mixing in theatrical circles.

It could be said that those wishing to live imperfect lives must first become perfectionists. In 1919 Fox made a blunder and received eight months' hard labour for forgery. The very next year he made a far worse blunder: he used the names of wealthy people to 'victimize' London shops, and was put away for six months.

This case marked another turning point in his life. It cost him a large number of friends and served as a warning to others. Although it did bring the Leslie family back into the picture and, in memory of his kindness to old Sir John, they arranged for the prodigal to have carpentry lessons.

Fox emerged from prison not a carpenter but a medical student – or, if that didn't meet the situation, a dog breeder, Old Etonian, farmer or pilot. And to celebrate his release, he had Mrs Fox come with him on a round of the best hotels. A luxurious life while it lasted.

Hotel fraud saw him jailed for a year in 1922. Fraud and larceny for another year – this time with hard labour – in 1924.

Life was getting tougher. The bloom of his youth was gone, and his *modus operandi* was now fairly well known to detectives such as that unmitigated swine Hambrook.

But while there was Mother, there was always a welcome and a place to lay one's head. Mrs Fox hadn't been doing all that badly: for years she'd lived in a flat costing as much a month as many middle-class couples were spending on a mortgage for a house. And the photograph of her on the mantelpiece, showing the same high, domed forehead as her Sidney, looked bold and prosperous enough, what with the *lorgnette* and yes, the fox-tailed fur stole. (Just how Mrs Fox supplemented her 10s pension is obscure; it can't really have been solely by being a cook and a char and accepting handouts, as the records suggest.)

Time passed. Fox managed to keep a low profile, and the Leslie family were no doubt pleased to see his name no longer in the papers. His mother started running a boarding house.

Then something dreadful happened to Mrs Fox in 1926. She began to fall about the place, and her movements became slow and awkward. Her hands shook and her mouth sometimes refused to utter words correctly. Sir Bernard Spilsbury later guessed that she had *paralysis agitans* – which is better known today as Parkinson's disease.

This was followed by something rather wonderful in 1927. Mrs Fox became bosom friends with Mrs Morse, who was the Australian wife of a captain in the Merchant Navy, then sailing the seas in the Far East. Mrs Morse was a stranger to England, and very lonely, despite being quite well-to-do. To her delight, dear Mrs Fox had no prejudices about Colonials on a three-year furlough, and it was only sensible that they should take a flat together in Southsea.

Fox fiddled himself a job with a nearby insurance company and moved in with the ladies, who were much relieved to have a man about the house.

And such a man as this: so young, so charming, so worldly and so *incredibly* romantic!

Mrs Morse's relief knew no bounds when, gritting his teeth,

as he was later to report, Fox committed an act of orthodox
intercourse on her middle-aged body. About as often as was
absolutely necessary to convince the sea widow that here at
last was the love of her life.

Conviction did not, however, bring with it large dividends.

Mrs Fox found it easy to 'borrow' small sums when she
pleased, but all her son got was talk of divorce and – way off
in the future – a blissful marriage.

Having already treated Mrs Morse with ruthless and cold-
blooded cruelty, of which she was still unaware, Fox presumably required very little adjustment to the idea of killing
her.

Here the bare facts can speak for themselves. He had Mrs
Morse make out her will in his favour. He insured her life for
£3,000. He was the first person in her gas-filled bedroom – after
she'd crawled to the window to scream for help.

And he had an immediate explanation for how his beloved
had so nearly met her death.

She may have been under the impression that the flat was
all-electric *but*, if one looked down behind her chest of
drawers, there was a gas tap set in the wall. In point of fact,
the landlady had warned him about it, and that was how he'd
known exactly where to stop the flow. His sweet silly-billy
must have accidentally turned the tap on herself, by banging
the drawers about before she went to bed. What she really
needed now, of course, was a good, strong cup of tea.

In all probability, Mrs Morse was preoccupied at that
moment with thoughts of her husband, to whom she'd written
to say her body and soul had been claimed by one more
worthy.

Not long afterwards, Mrs Fox and Mr Fox took their leave,
and moved into other lodgings. Mrs Morse, much the poorer
for their friendship, then discovered she was even poorer than
she thought: a locked drawer had been forced open and some
jewellery stolen.

Nobody likes to think that someone has tried to kill them
for their possessions, and so the theft appears to be the only
thing Mrs Morse actually reported to the police, half-hoping,
probably, that it'd been the work of someone other than her
lover.

Fox was on the run. He took his mother to Portsmouth that
Christmas and left her in the care of his eldest half-brother,

who was a monitor at a mental home.

During January of the new year, Fox returned and moved his mother into lodgings, without having told his brother of his intentions.

Then he went to ground.

On February 20, Mrs Fox was admitted to the workhouse at St Mary's Infirmary, Portsmouth, as a destitute person, but when her condition was observed, the authorities moved her into the infirmary itself. Although her mind and appetite were as lively as ever, she was very feeble and could only just shuffle about.

In March, Fox began to serve a 15-month sentence for the theft of Mrs Morse's jewellery. It was before this trial that he told his counsel that sleeping with a woman was something abhorrent to his nature – from which the line of his defence can be readily assumed.

Once the fact of Fox's treachery was proved beyond doubt, the unfortunate Mrs Morse – whose husband was suing for divorce – left for Australia. Some sources say that this was when she tore up her will, others say she revoked it after the gas incident; there is very little about Mrs Morse and her reactions to the family Fox. But she did leave him one small legacy: a passing mention of the gas-filled room, which the police were to recall almost two years later.

Fox behaved himself in prison and served only a year. As soon as he came out, he released Mrs Fox from her hospital bed on March 27, 1929, and they began their wanderings from hotel to hotel.

This is the point at which the jury picked up the story.

In his opening speech for the prosecution, the Attorney-General, Sir William Jowitt, told them practically everything they would know about the past history of the accused and his alleged victim before a verdict was reached. Some details were added later by minor witnesses – and by Fox himself – but this was really all it came down to:

Sidney Harry Fox: age 31, unemployed bachelor receiving 8s disability pension; native of Great Fransham; some military service, confined to British Isles. (Fox would admit to defrauding a few hotels since taking his mother from hospital. The references to Mrs Morse would be provokingly enigmatic.)

Wardrobe at time of alleged offence: what he stood up in.

Not much for the jury to work on there, but such are the rules of evidence – most merciful, as Mr Justice Avory said.

Mrs Rosaline Fox: age 63, widow receiving 10s war pension; native of Great Fransham; married signalman and had four sons: eldest a witness, second son died in action, third son killed in munitions explosion, fourth son in the dock. Occupied various flats and houses in London and Southsea; worked as char, cook and boarding-house keeper; developed *paralysis agitans* in 1926; admitted destitute and ill to St Mary's Infirmary in February, 1928; taken from there by fourth son in March, 1929; became party to hotel frauds, and visited war graves in France.

Wardrobe at time of death: overcoat, small fur, combination, vest, two pairs of stockings, a pair of shoes, two stockinette dresses, worn one over the other.

And what a very sad, dreary life that sounded.

But to continue the narrative, piecing it together from the evidence of more than fifty witnesses who did not, of course, appear in chronological order.

On April 21, while in Norwich, Mrs Fox had Sidney take down her will on a form from the stationer's, which he did in his very handsome script. Fox always said it was at her dictation, anyway.

In this will she asked that gifts should be made from her belongings to 'my dear friends Louise Baxter and Emma Young in token of their kindness and friendship'. Then came the punchline:

'To my (eldest) son, William Edward Fox, I leave the sum of one farthing, and sincerely hope that he will never want his mother; the remainder to my son, Sidney Harry Fox, for his own use and benefit absolutely.'

And she signed it twice, very shakily.

Nine days later, Fox took out the first accident policy on her life, and asked a lot of questions about what an accident might involve – food poisoning was just one of his queried ideas. Violent, external and visible means was the answer.

He and his mother carried on with their travels and, the prudent traveller he was, Fox carried on buying short-term accident cover – on one occasion for himself. They went to

France and sent a postcard back to a landlady they knew in London.

Then it was home again, to the Grand Hotel at Dover, the Royal Pavilion at Folkestone, and the County Hotel, Canterbury, which they left bearing a small brown-paper parcel, and pursued by the porter.

A parcel that had disappeared by the following evening when they finally arrived at the Hotel Metropole. They were greeted at the reception window by the kindly Miss Vera Hopper, and were given the two single rooms Fox requested. Later that evening he explained they were on their way to a new home at Lyndhurst, and had sent their luggage on ahead of them. He also asked Miss Hopper to place a small package in the hotel safe.

Miss Hopper apparently thought little about this, but the manager, Mr Harding, began to take a mild interest in Fox from that moment. Later, when Miss Hopper handed it back, and the guest checked the contents, she saw it was 'only papers'; this confirmed Mr Harding's suspicions of a swindler's ploy, as he was to tell the court. (Ironically, and this the court never knew, those *were* valuable papers in Fox's eyes: one was Mrs Morse's will, and the other the policy on her life.)

The Fox family didn't leave the next morning as they'd said they would. Fox had people he wanted to see in the district, he confided to Miss Hopper, with whom he had a succession of friendly if condescending chats. Mr Harding had wanted to give him his bill, but Fox blocked this insinuation by asking for it first. Something which, incidentally, he did every day.

On Friday – they'd been there since Wednesday, and Mrs Fox was eating heartily – Fox asked Mr Harding to recommend a solicitor in Margate. Then he went to Ramsgate and spent 2s on insuring his mother for £1,000 in the event of her accidental death by external means.

Back at reception, he worked on Miss Hopper with his story of the pilgrimage to the war graves, and with details of his mother's feeble constitution. Miss Hopper offered Mrs Fox the loan of her own fur coat to travel in, but Fox wouldn't hear of it. Presumably, his pawn-shop days were over.

The filthy rich must have been something of a reality in 1930, because the chambermaid's evidence would make it clear that she didn't find the Fox couple remarkable. She handed Mrs Fox her food-sticky teeth every morning with

72

her tea, collected up her two dresses from the chair, cleaned her coat with petrol and, just as in the schoolboy joke, emptied her chamber, all with a good-naturedness that must have cheered Fox immensely.

Then on Sunday Mrs Fox apparently became ill and Dr Cecil Austin was called in by Mr Harding. Dr Austin prescribed a tonic; Mr Harding moved Mrs Fox into a room with a gas fire; and a page boy was sent to the chemist's. Fox tried to buy another bottle of the tonic that night with a cheque forged in his mother's name, but the chemist refused it – on the grounds that the sheet of hotel notepaper he'd used bore only one penny stamp.

Fox tried again with two penny stamps in the morning: no good, the medicine would be made up, but it was to be a cash transaction. The girl assistant, left on her own at lunchtime, didn't know this; she gave Fox two bottles of tonic, one bottle of cascara tablets, and £1 16s change from the cheque which her employer had already approved.

This was the ticket to London that Fox needed in order to extend accident cover on his mother until the unusual time of midnight on the coming Wednesday (it was customary for cover to run from noon to noon). Fox had made many such short-term extensions before on policies which had since lapsed entirely, and they cost very little; he'd also bought dozens of one-day policies, always with the excuse that his Mama wouldn't travel by train without protection. This is, of course, another reminder of life before the NHS.

The chambermaid, having been tipped a hefty 7s 6d, kept an eye on Mrs Fox while he was away, and saw that the devoted son had left some grapes. Miss Hopper had a call from London that night, and was able to tell Fox that all was well and not to worry himself so about the old dear.

On Tuesday morning, Fox went through an elaborate Mahonesque routine of sending himself a bogus telephone message through a former London landlady – the same person who'd been sent the postcard from France. The message was that Mrs Fox was ill, and he was wanted urgently at her bedside; the plan was to raise a small loan, ostensibly for the train fare. It didn't work.

With a pound at most in his pocket, Fox returned to the Metropole late that same night.

Early next morning, the morning of that fateful Wednesday,

the chambermaid found Mrs Fox's teeth on the carpet. She also discovered that Mrs Fox had bolted the connecting door to Room 67. These were things one remembered, rather than thought about at the time.

That evening the barmaid in the saloon lounge politely listened to another of Mr Fox's stories. On the Sunday he'd told her that Dr Austin had been drunk while examining Mrs Fox, and that the chemist had watered down the prescription. In fact, according to Fox, Dr Austin had waggled his hands rudely and said: 'You are all right, old lady! Bogey, bogey!' This time the news was that they were leaving for Lyndhurst in the morning. 'Mother and I have had a sham fight,' said Fox, 'which shows she is well.'

The chambermaid saw Mrs Fox reading a newspaper in Room 66 just before Fox fetched his mother down to dinner.

The waitress, Mrs Bugg, served Mrs Fox a mixed grill, which was washed down by half a pint of beer. That was the last time she was seen alive by the hotel staff.

Fox nipped out later and bought a half-bottle of port at another hotel, which he took up to his mother's room, together with a newspaper borrowed from the barmaid. Then he returned to the saloon lounge, had a few drinks, and moved on at closing-time for a final half-pint in the lower bar.

Mr Harding saw Fox coming away from this bar at about 10.40 p.m. He expected the usual bit of smooth chatter, but the guest froze on seeing him, said nothing, and suddenly dashed past and up the stairs.

Fox was back on those same stairs an hour later, dressed in his vest and shouting for help.

'I appealed to the people around me to get her out of the smoke,' Mr Samuel Hopkins, the doughty commercial traveller told the court. 'I was feeling very bad. The accused played no part in helping me to remove his mother. I was ill for three weeks afterwards.'

No fireman would have been surprised to hear that – today the use of breathing apparatus in such a situation is mandatory. Mr Hopkins had inhaled considerable quantities of soot, besides a toxic amount of carbon monoxide, and had suffered shock.

'We are all agreed you did a very plucky action,' said Sir Henry Curtis-Bennett. 'You are all right now, I hope?'

'Yes. I am still a little nervous, and my legs give me a little pain if I am on them too much.'

Mrs Fox had looked dead to Mr Henry Miller, one of several commercial travellers who had responded to that appeal.

'Have you seen a person die?' asked Mr Cassels.

And received a tacit reply from a veteran of the trenches.

Then came the turn of the professional observers, although Dr Cecil C. Austin hardly distinguished himself as such.

His memories of the Sunday visit to Mrs Fox's bedside were rather vague. He didn't remember being told she'd fainted. He thought she might have been in a nightgown. But he was certain he hadn't gone 'Bogey, bogey!'

As for the emergency call on the Wednesday night, there wasn't much he could say about that either. The corpse's very flushed face had led him to diagnose shock and suffocation.

'I went up to Room 66, but I only made a casual examination,' he said. 'I noticed the chair was burned.'

Finally, Mr Justice Rowlatt put this to him: 'You did not see anything remarkable about the lady at all. She was simply dead, and that was the long and short of it?'

'Yes,' agreed Dr Austin.

His colleague, Dr Robert W. Nichol, gave a detailed description of everything he had seen and done, right down to examining the handbag. But he hadn't examined Mrs Fox because, without an invitation from Dr Austin, that would not have been medical etiquette.

'Would it be right to say that Mrs Fox's face was composed, pale, and presented no special significance?' Mr Cassels inquired, planting the first half of a trick question.

'It would.'

Dr Nichol went on to say that he had not been satisfied with the given cause of death, and would himself have ordered a post-mortem. He had seen victims of suffocation and gassing, but candidly admitted that his medical opinions were based on textbooks.

Anyone can be wise after an event. Yet it is only fair to note how Dr Nichol's subconscious seems to have reacted at the time: he brought up the matter of an inquest, a query about insurance, and the need for a solicitor, all within an hour of the fire.

His cross-examination closed with Mr Cassels springing the

other half of that question:

'You were not answering "out of the book" when you said that the face was pale, composed, and presented no special significance?'

'I think,' Dr Nichol replied evenly, 'you would get that answer from anyone who saw the body.'

With the evidence of Dr Austin and one police witness excepted, he was quite right.

The very curious features of the fire were outlined for the jury. It had been under the armchair and had spread *towards* the fender, leaving a six-inch gap of unburned carpet. A cane chair, with one leg burned, had been found near the window – a good distance away. The charred remains of the *Evening Standard* and a French newspaper had been discovered on the floor.

The innocent explanation ran something like this: port-befuddled Mrs Fox had dropped the newspapers beside her armchair before retiring, and they had formed a 'bridge' across to the gas fire – or, alternatively, she had left her under-clothes where they would have the same effect. The fire had crept across to beneath the armchair, set alight the horse-hair stuffing, and had burned a hole through to the floor-boards.

But experiments had not supported this theory.

All sort of ways of burning a hole through the carpet had been tried, but they'd been successful only when petrol was used. Moreover, the combination couldn't have become hot enough to ignite; and if the cane chair had been used as a clothes horse, then its back and not its leg would have been burned.

There were other factors to be taken into consideration as well. This same befuddled Mrs Fox, so careless with her underclothes, had – for the first time ever – hung her dresses up neatly behind the door. If normality was the keynote, then why was Mrs Fox's pillow on the locker next to her bed? – why were her teeth across in the washbasin? And how had the cane chair, which nobody remembered moving, made its way across the room?

The Chief Officer of the Margate Fire Brigade, Mr Harry Hammond, told the court that he'd revised his ideas about the fire after trying to simulate it himself.

'I cannot find any means of it being an accidental fire,' he said in his examination-in-chief.

At Mr Cassels' request, Mr Hammond put a match to some horse-hair stuffing – after a mild objection from the judge. When lit from below, it tainted the court with a thick, pungent smoke.

Lieutenant-Colonel C. J. Fox, a fire expert, then stepped into the witness box and did an about-turn, without having said a word. The defence objected to his giving an opinion on what was a matter for the jury.

So much for the fire. The insurance side of things had also been dealt with at length – as well as in a nutshell by Mr Robert Hawkins, claims assessor of the Ocean Accident and Guarantee Corporation Ltd., whose entire evidence was:

'There were a number of one-day policies taken out on the life of the deceased, Mrs Rosaline Fox, the last of which expired at midnight on the 23rd October. A claim was received. Inquiries were made, and the claim is still outstanding.'

The trial was notable for the unusually active role played by the jury, which interrupted the proceedings several times with questions of its own. The second of these was: 'Can we be told whether Mrs Fox or the accused could speak French?'

At the end of the fourth day, a witness was sworn in who would surely know the answer: Mr William Edward Fox, 41, of Portsmouth, the inheritor of one farthing.

'I first heard of her death on November 5 by seeing it in a newspaper,' Mr Fox said, before being asked to identify the handwriting on various documents.

They seemed to be all in his brother's hand – 'Her handwriting in recent years was very, very shaky.'

But she had apparently written some of the will, and she'd signed it. Even if Mr Fox knew of his half-brother's conviction for forgery, he was not, of course, able to refer to this.

Just before an adjournment, he said: 'As far as I know, my mother had no knowledge of the French language.'

Mr Cassels began his cross-examination by asking when Mr Fox had last lived with his mother – apart from the time she'd spent as a guest during the Christmas period in 1927.

'I have not lived in the same house since 1908.'

'Had there been some family differences?'

The hospital attendant paused before saying: 'In what way do you mean?'

'That there had been differences between your part of the family, on the one hand, and your mother on the other?'

'Not my mother.'

Mrs Fox had been rather difficult to manage while staying over Christmas because of her frequent falls. She had shuffled about, and her arms hadn't been strong enough to help her out of a chair without assistance.

'She could eat well?'

'Very well indeed,' affirmed Mr Fox.

His mother had been depressed, not playful as suggested, and he'd never seen her have a 'sham fight' with the accused. Most of Mr Fox's evidence had the same clipped quality as that given by Miss Emily Bealby Kaye's sister, and it spoke volumes between the lines.

'Did you know your brother was going to take your mother [away permanently] when he took her out of your house?'

'No, but I found she had gone to a Mrs Taylor in Neville Road, Copnor, Portsmouth.'

'And she was in a very feeble condition?'

'Yes.'

'Do you know your mother was an inmate of an institution in Portsmouth?'

'Yes.'

'And did you visit her there?'

'No.'

'Have you had any letters from her since she was in that institution?'

'No.'

'She did not communicate with you very much?'

'No,' said William Edward, 'very little.'

Anyone who had sat through the trial of the poultry farmer, Norman Thorne, could be forgiven a deep sigh over the medical evidence in the Fox case. Once again Sir Bernard Spilsbury had seen the corpse while it was still relatively fresh, and once again the other experts hadn't. Five years later, almost to the very day, the old arguments went on.

Not that they were entirely without interest: Sir Bernard produced a model of the human mouth and throat to show the jury how he'd stumbled (as it were) on what he believed was the cause of death.

While searching in vain for soot in the air passages, he'd

found a large bruise the size of a half-crown at the back of the larynx; a bruise made by 'mechanical violence'.

This had led to the discovery of another bruise, this time invisible to the naked eye, situated about halfway along Mrs Fox's tongue. It had been caused – for want of any other explanation – by the lower denture being forced against the upper denture during strangulation.

That there hadn't been any external signs of violence didn't necessarily mean anything.

And so Dr Austin had been completely wrong: Mrs Fox hadn't died of shock, suffocation or, as the defence experts would suggest, heart failure. She'd been strangled by hand before the fire got going, and possibly while asleep.

The snag was that besides Spilsbury only the Chief Constable of Norfolk had seen the 'half-crown' bruise – decomposition having set in very rapidly after the exhumation.

Mr Cassels made the most of this, and said: 'The bruise at the back of the larynx might easily have been a mark of putrefaction?'

'It was a bruise, and nothing else,' replied Spilsbury. 'There are no two opinions about it. If it had been putrefaction, the mark would not have been red in colour, but green.'

The fact that the delicate hyoid bone hadn't been fractured was also made a major issue, but Spilsbury could produce cases in which this anchor for the tongue had remained intact despite manual strangulation.

As for the suggestion of heart failure, brought on by a sudden fright that had made Mrs Fox wet her bed and try to heave herself out of it, she'd been protected against such by her *paralysis agitans* – she just couldn't have moved quickly if she tried.

For his final question, Mr Cassels asked: 'In your experience of strangulation cases, have you ever known of a case with fewer signs than this?'

'No, I have not,' Spilsbury agreed.

Dr Henry D. Weir, pathologist to the National Hospital for Diseases of the Heart, the Crown's last witness, would have gone along with the heart-failure theory – but for the bruises. In his opinion, strangulation had brought on a fatal collapse.

Both defence experts were for heart failure produced by shock.

'In manual strangulation,' said Professor Sydney Smith,

the Scots pathologist, 'marks would be found of the fingers on the surface of the skin of the neck – the indentation of nails and pressure of the tips of the fingers.'

Dr Brontë, a very distant relation of the famous sisters, who looked upon Spilsbury as some form of 'Wuthering Heights' he meant to conquer, was more blunt than that.

'I don't see how bruising of the inner tissues could occur without bruising of the tissues themselves,' he said.

After an undignified clash with the Attorney-General, Dr Brontë had to admit: 'I cannot say what Sir Bernard Spilsbury saw.' And that was the crux of the matter.

On top of which, to judge from any textbook on forensic medicine today, Professor Smith and Dr Brontë were not so much at variance with Spilsbury as plain wrong in their ideas about the damage 'invariably' caused by manual strangulation. Here is the relevant paragraph from *Glaister's Medical Jurisprudence and Toxicology*, published by Churchill Livingstone in 1973:

'The absence of bruising upon the skin, when deep-seated bruising is present, can be accounted for by the maintenance of pressure until death has supervened, since compression of the skin will empty the vessels in it during life, and the heart may have ceased to beat before the pressure has been removed.'

For a mildly bizarre example of how force can leave very little in the way of 'signs of violence', one can turn to *The Essentials of Forensic Medicine*, by Professor C. J. Polson:

'There is no doubt about the pressure he [the killer of an army matron] had exerted with his hand on her neck before he applied her stocking, because when examined he had a severe sprain of the thumb. Yet the only external mark left was an indefinite circular abrasion on the front of her neck.'

But for a reminder of the age in which Fox's trial took place, we have only to refer to a reply Sir Bernard gave to one of Mr Cassels' inquiries:

'Did you examine the mucous lining of the nose?'

'No, because every person has a deposit of soot in the nose ...'

Lightning struck unexpectedly while Sidney Harry Fox was in the witness box on the seventh day of his trial. There was a 'terrific thunderclap', and the courtroom darkened.

Fox didn't turn a hair. Obviously the sound hadn't the

same guilt associations for him as it had held for Mahon, yet it did startle everyone else, and this imperturbability was taken as further proof of a cold-blooded killer's nerve – or so some accounts claim. Not once did he lose his air of quiet confidence, not even when the actual words he used made it clear he was rattled, and his business-like tone was a definite mistake. His worst mistake was, of course, electing to give evidence at all, but he'd spent his life talking his way out of trouble, and his conceit got the better of him.

Right at the start he began working on his 'devoted son' image, with a reference to his mother's stay in the infirmary: 'When I went to get her out, she was very much grieved that her eldest son had never been to see her.' And he followed this up with: 'I was with my mother from then onwards until the day she died. I looked after her.'

'What,' asked Mr Cassels, 'was the feeling between you and your mother?'

'Well, excellent – the ordinary feeling between mother and son,' replied Fox, only he gave it the flatness of a clinical observation. 'I loved her', would have been a lot simpler, too.

His mother's 'one desire' had been to visit the war grave in France, and they had also visited the grave of a cousin, Cecil Reginald Fox. (Someone of whom his half-brother had never heard – it's worth noting that Cecil and Reginald were the first names of the two dead Fox brothers.)

Mr Cassels grasped a thistle: 'Tell me, Fox, did you sometimes leave hotels without paying?'

'Yes.'

'Did you find that at all difficult to do?'

'No.'

'You had no luggage?'

'No.'

Then surely the hoteliers had been as much to blame, and nobody could say that Fox was totally incapable of telling the truth. Not much of a gain against the fact that the accused was a self-confessed fraud, but Mr Cassels could only do his best.

Fox explained that his mother's illness had delayed their departure, but he'd used the time to go up to London in the hope of borrowing money for their hotel bill. Then a cramp in his leg – the result of a fracture in 1926 – had caused a further delay.

On the Wednesday night, he had placed the grapes and newspaper on the cane chair in front of the fire, where she was sitting. They'd just shared the half-bottle of port together. He had taken off her dress for her, wrapped her in an eider-down, and kissed her goodnight.

Later, after realizing her room was filled with smoke, he had gone to get help.

'I was choking and all that, and, being lame, I made the best effort I could. I ran downstairs, which I think I did very quickly.'

Not only that, but he'd got himself just inside the door of Room 66 when Mr Hopkins began dragging his mother out.

He wasn't too sure of what had happened next: 'I was then in a state of collapse. The smoke was very thick in the corridor, making it difficult to see.'

The alleged £24 in the handbag was another nettle to be grasped and, hopefully, squeezed dry.

'Why did you raise that question?' asked Mr Cassels, after being told that it had contained *some* money, but not the amount mentioned.

'Because I did not want anyone to think we were staying at the hotel without money,' answered Fox.

The accident policies also needed some explaining, even if they had been his mother's own idea.

'She wished to have her policy really in case she met with an accident in a bus smash, or slipped in the street, so that she could get good medical treatment. She had fallen in the street once and broken her foot, and the expenses incurred were fairly heavy.'

A little later his counsel said: 'What was the insurance for yourself and your mother on 23rd October (the Wednesday)?'

'Three thousand pounds in event of death, £18 a week if she had been disabled [a week at the Metropole for both of them cost far less than that], probably £9 a week if only partially disabled.'

The £2,000 policy had been extended until midnight on Wednesday because Fox and his mother had originally intended travelling that day. Ironically, the extension hadn't cost anything because the period involved was a mere twelve hours.

'With regard to these sham fights you had with your mother,' said Mr Cassels, 'they were just playfulness – you were doing your best to cheer her up?'

'Yes, we often played together. It used to amuse her.'

With a smile, Fox began to demonstrate: 'I would sometimes hold her hands – she was rather strong in her arms – and
I would let her purposely release herself.'

How unpleasant that sounded in the context of the soiled
sheet.

The Attorney-General rose and had Fox show himself for a
clumsy liar with just two questions.

'How much money had you on the evening of 23rd October?'

'I cannot say exactly, but approximately a pound.'

'Had your mother any money?'

'So far as I know, she had no money.'

In his eagerness to 'come clean' over an apparent irrel-
evancy, Fox tripped right over what he'd said to Mr Cassels
about the handbag. But his face didn't give anything away.

Sir William Jowitt continued to cross-examine him about
the family finances, and Fox admitted to forging the cheque
presented at the chemist's shop.

'Did you anticipate trouble with that cheque?'

'No, not if the money was repaid,' said the accused, adding
by way of a polite reminder: 'It was, in fact, repaid.'

'It was repaid by money you borrowed from your solicitor.'

'Yes.'

'Did you borrow the money from your solicitor by telling
him a pack of lies?'

'I may have told him one or two untruths.'

Mahon had favoured that subtle distinction, too – with
about as much success.

'Did you tell him lies?'

'Yes.'

Gradually Fox became boxed into a corner, and stated that
for two months he and his mother had been living far above
their weekly pension money.

'You had no other income?' asked Sir William.

'My mother had money besides from friends,' Fox replied
casually. 'She had had gifts and loans from a friend, Mrs
Morse.'

The jury may have wondered then why several people looked
up sharply.

'Who is Mrs Morse?'

'She is a very well-to-do Australian lady,' said Fox. 'She was over here for three years, and lived with us whilst at Southsea practically the whole time. She returned to Australia at the end of last year.'

'Did she return to Australia shortly after or shortly before your mother's death?'

'I don't know the day she sailed.'

Fox was evidently quite pleased with the effect these disclosures might have on the jury. It gave his mother a certain status, and it – but he hadn't reckoned on this being a game two could play.

'You know a good deal about Mrs Morse?' Sir William inquired in a neutral tone.

'I do. She has lived with us.'

And back came the ball, bouncing hard:

'She was a married woman living apart from her husband, Captain Morse?'

'Yes, he has business abroad.'

'And Captain Morse had instituted divorce proceedings against his wife?'

'Yes.'

'And you have been cited as co-respondent?'

'Yes, I have had the papers,' said Fox, managing to keep matter-of-fact.

Then he revealed that Mrs Morse had left him 'moneys' in her will, and that he had once, in his capacity as an insurance agent, sold her a policy at her request.

'Did you go into room No. 66 after the fire?' asked the Attorney-General, hinting at a repetition of what had happened once before – although only Fox was meant to get the point of this, one assumes.

Twice, was the answer; it didn't add anything.

Fox's need to adapt his tales to maintain their plausibility often distracted him from the real reason he was being questioned on certain points. He had already linked his mother's name with Lady Paget to give the impression Mrs Fox rubbed shoulders with the aristocracy, and to imply that accidents will happen in the best-regulated families. Now he had to show how a woman from the workhouse could claim such acquaintanceship, and in his haste to deal with the apparent lie, he quite overlooked the implication.

'Some fortnight before your mother's death, did the death

of Walburgar, Lady Paget, take place?'

'Yes.'

'She was an old lady who died as the result of a fire?'

'I never met Lady Paget – I don't know,' replied Fox, needing a moment to adjust.

'Is that what the papers said?'

'Yes; she was reading a newspaper in front of the fire when her dress caught fire. My mother read it out to me.'

'Did that make some impression on your mind?'

'No. I did not know Lady Paget. My mother knew her; they had met at the Red Cross.'

Fox had missed the point, but Sir William made it explicit by asking if he hadn't mentioned the strange coincidence to Dr Nichol after the hotel fire. Yes, he had.

And no, he hadn't moved the cane chair.

Then the Attorney-General began a sequence of questions which led to a reply that shocked the court and, in the opinion of many who were present, dropped the noose over Fox's head. Sir William returned to the night of the fire, and to what Fox had done after being awakened by the smoke seeping into his bedroom.

'Did you realize, when you opened the communicating door, that the atmosphere in the room was such as would probably suffocate anybody inside?'

'If I had stayed in three or four moments, I should have been suffocated.'

'So that you must have been greatly apprehensive for your mother?'

'I was,' asserted the devoted son.

'Fox, you closed the door?'

'It is quite possible I did.'

'Can you explain to me,' said Sir William, 'why it was you closed the door – instead of flinging it wide open?'

Fox responded glibly: 'My explanation for that now is that the smoke should not spread into the hotel.'

And – according to Miss F. Tennyson Jesse – 'Such a gasp went up from the crowded courtroom while everyone present drew in a breath of horror, as to be definitely audible.'

The cross-examination could well have stopped right there. Miss Tennyson Jesse records, in her introduction to the *Notable British Trials* volume on Fox, that his demeanour remained 'perfectly calm' until the end of the ordeal, but that only makes his behaviour seem even more unnatural.

Fox had told the barmaid he'd closed the door, and there was no escaping from that fact, however vague his recollection suddenly became. Nor could he get around having left the passage door closed on his way downstairs.

'It is all very well trying to pin me down to details,' he admonished the Attorney-General, 'but I don't hardly remember what I did do. I was agitated on discovering the hotel on fire.'

Sir William would have thought it was the knowledge that his mother was in the room that had caused his agitation.

'Certainly.'

'Which is it now?'

'I don't remember,' said Fox, and complained again about being expected to recall everything that occurred.

As for the dresses being behind the door, that was simple: he had put them there – although he'd told the coroner that Mrs Fox had been fully dressed when he last saw her. This was because he didn't want everyone to know he helped her undress.

'Do you remember your mother having a French newspaper?'

'No. She had one or two circulars about motor coaches which had been given to her in France. She had them in her bag.'

'Does it strike you as an extraordinary coincidence that a month later there should be found, among the charred paper, some French paper?' asked Sir William.

'If it *was* a French newspaper, I cannot account for it being there.'

Fox's evidence about the insurance policies had been a trifle misleading – one of them took care of injuries, but the other paid up only in the event of death, as the Attorney-General went on to remind the jury.

'Is the truth about these policies that you were desperately hard up for money?'

'I do not agree.'

'That you knew the life you were leading could only come to one end, and that quickly?'

'No,' said Fox. 'It would have ended the same day, because we were going to London.'

'That Mrs Morse had gone to Australia, and you wanted to

go to Australia?'

'I did not want to go to Australia, and I should never have gone in my mother's lifetime.'

'If your mother had died you were going there?'

'That was my intention.'

For those who knew more than the jury did about Mrs Morse, the irony of this exchange must have been acute – especially when they heard Fox's next reply.

'Would you have gone to Australia if you could have raised the fare?'

'I should probably have been there by now.'

It remained only to ask: 'Did you desperately want to get the money to pay your fare to Australia?'

'Certainly not,' Fox retorted.

And then for Sir William to say, after a quick succession of hammer-blow accusations: 'Did you destroy your mother on the night of 23rd October in order that you might reap £3,000 from those insurance policies?'

'Most certainly not! It is a horrible suggestion – horrible.'

Out came the handkerchief and Fox dabbed at his eyes, while Mr Cassels stood up to make his brief re-examination.

The first question was: 'Did you know that if you were to strangle a woman in her bed, you could do it without leaving a mark?'

'No.'

The last question gave Fox an opportunity to refute the idea he'd deliberately left his mother to suffocate.

'Never. If I closed the door, it was in the panic of rushing away to get help.'

With that, the prisoner returned to the dock.

In his closing speech for the defence, Mr Cassels concentrated on the doubts raised over the 'half-crown' bruise, and on how preposterous it seemed that Fox should choose the worst possible moment to fake his mother's 'fatal accident'. She had, after all, been worth £4,000 on the day they arrived at the Hotel Metropole, and that extra £1,000 could have been very handy.

The Attorney-General left Lewes at lunch-time to attend other matters, and the closing speech for the Crown was made by Sir Henry Curtis-Bennett.

Mrs Fox's interest in accident insurance, Sir Henry pointed

out, had not been in evidence until after she'd made out her will. He wasn't suggesting that Fox had originally intended to murder her, but it was a factor worth thinking about.

'Perhaps he thought she might be killed in some accidental way which was not criminal, and he took steps to see, if that did take place, that she would be worth some money.'

There was an hour – from 10.40 to 11.40 p.m. – about which nobody knew anything. If the fire had not been accidental, then there was only one person who could have lit it.

'I should point out on the morning of 24th October the accused said he was going to Australia, where a woman he was fond of – who had made a will leaving him money – had gone. On 23rd October he had not a farthing to take him to Australia, and this poor old lady, in the condition in which she was, had no money.'

And finally, said Sir Henry, it wasn't necessary for the Crown to prove precisely how Mrs Fox had died, but simply that she had been murdered by her youngest son.

'It is murder or nothing,' Mr Justice Rowlatt told the jury when he began his summing-up on the ninth day of the trial.

Three things of a positive nature had to be said about the accused. Fox had frankly admitted defrauding the hotels. Fox had not asked for a room with a gas fire. If Fox had, in fact, strangled his mother and then lit the fire before the other guests were in bed, then he'd taken a very big risk – Mr Hopkins and his colleagues could have intervened too early.

Everything else the judge had to say went the other way. A venerable Edwardian in appearance, he was nonetheless given to direct statements that could leave some present-day justices seeming very fuddyduddy.

'It is one thing to plot this kind of thing, and another to find an opportunity for it,' he said, referring to the £1,000 drop in Mrs Fox's market value that had been stressed by the defence. 'The nerve might fail, y'know.'

As for certain bewildering aspects of the case, it was true that 'Murderers do funny things', and while the jury should attempt to rationalize some of them, they weren't to 'push it too far' – the accused had, after all, done a lot of thinking on his feet.

The court adjourned at 1.11 p.m. to await the verdict. After an hour and ten minutes, the jury sent for the deceased's dentures. They were very probably requested by the juror who had tackled Spilsbury about them in person during someone else's evidence. Now this juror had a theory that the jaw alone could have . . .

Barely fifteen minutes later, Sidney Harry Fox was sentenced to death.

'My lord, I never murdered my mother,' he said with a forlorn, 'crooning' inflection, as he touched a hand to the neat knot in his tie.

And a woman in the gallery cried out: 'If his own mother was here, she would forgive him!'

Silly woman.

His own mother was there, albeit in a very limited way: part of her voicebox had been providing silent testimony of matricide on the exhibits table all along.

Then the wild rumours started.

And they didn't come any wilder than the widespread belief that Mrs Fox had been, not his mother, but his mistress. Like a suspense drama which seems convincing enough at the time, yet falls apart the instant the curtain drops, the nine-day trial suddenly failed to make sense any longer and the theorizing became a free-for-all. So what if that sounded fantastic – wasn't it a fantastic suggestion that an *ex-insurance clerk* should risk his neck in such an obvious way?

Of course it was. But ignoring the facts – even though one had a sneaking feeling a lot of them had been twisted – was not going to solve any mysteries.

The mystery of what had made Fox encumber himself with an ageing invalid, when he could have patently done so much better on his own, was one which teased at everyone's imagination. A typical explanation went like this:

Mummy's boy had been genuinely fond of his mother, for whom he had much to thank, and had cared for her as best he could. Until her worsening condition, and their declining fortunes, had driven him to commit a clumsy mercy-killing with 'waste not, want not' for his motto.

Miss Tennyson Jesse, who wrote her introduction to the Fox trial in 1934, was more cynical in her conclusions. She suggested that Mrs Fox had represented young Sidney's only remaining asset and, to paraphrase, he'd gone ahead and liquidated it. This does account for his having removed the poor old lady from the infirmary, where she was at least sure of a bed each night, and it seems to have been the generally accepted theory ever since.

But one could be more cynical still – and possibly arrive much closer to the truth of what really happened at the Hotel Metropole that fateful week.

Silver locks, trembling hands and an unsteady, shuffling walk: they all add up to our stock picture of the 'poor old lady' whom Sir Henry Curtis-Bennett described. An image of passive dependence, pathetic in its impotence and infantile greed, which can frighten us all when we dare to think that some day we could share her plight. And so we buy our endowment policies and thank God for the Welfare State.

We're forgetting how we laugh at the grandmother in the Giles cartoons – and *why* we laugh at her: because she's a delightfully wicked old woman, and some old people can be very wicked indeed. We're forgetting that Mrs Fox was only 63 – and merely 'old for her age' as the Attorney-General pointed out. We're forgetting that at 60 she was setting up house with Mrs Morse.

The way most accounts read – if they mention the captain's wife at all – would indicate that Mrs Fox was 'on to a good thing' there until her son came along and messed it all up. This tends to overlook rather a number of things.

Mrs Fox was in a desperate situation when that friendship was formed; she had become incapable of supporting herself any longer, Sidney couldn't be relied upon, William was unsympathetic, and the workhouse loomed ahead. These were the facts of the matter. It was also a fact that the friendship carried a three-year limit, and that hay had to be made while the Antipodean sun shone.

She must have agreed to Sidney joining the party. She must have known he wasn't a lady's man, and she must have known – in a flat that size – about the passionate romance with Mrs Morse. Finally, she must have known about the gas incident.

So much for what lies beyond reasonable doubt. Although surmise could take the matter further, without asking too much of the given situation. For instance, it doesn't seem unlikely that Mrs Morse treated her as a confidante, and discussed with Mrs Fox such important issues as the will, the £3,000 policy, and her forthcoming marriage to that marvellous young man, their very own Sidney.

And for something to ponder, there is the curious behaviour of the landlady. According to Fox, this Mrs Fleming had shown him the gas tap behind the chest of drawers in a room which wasn't his own – and yet, by implication, she hadn't said a thing about it when his mother and Mrs Morse moved in. One would have thought that whoever arranged the tenancy had received that warning.

Mrs Fox left that address in even more desperate straits than ever. The ruthless might suppose that the two-and-two of the gas incident had, however, given her a trump card – an ace she threatened to toss down at the nearest police station – should she ever want for a devoted son. (The *thoroughly* ruthless might feel that, having actually conspired for a £1,500 half-share, it was she who first applied a stranglehold by proposing to turn King's evidence.)

There is no way of knowing. Perhaps this was just a gnawing fear in Fox's mind – which is what, at the very least, another look at the evidence suggests.

The theft of the jewellery put Fox on the run. He dumped his mother with William Fox over Christmas – a season noted for the criminal opportunities it offers – and then got her away again as soon as possible to a 'secret' address. But no sooner had he placed her in lodgings than he was arrested, and she went into the workhouse.

What follows is one way in which the facts can be re-interpreted from there. Naturally other permutations are possible – mother and son could have made some sort of pact, for example – but that can be left to individual choice. Or rejection.

Fox spent a year inside, scheming his way back into Mrs Morse's affections, and worrying himself sick about what his mother might be letting slip – with his record, a conviction for attempted murder would have meant a very long stretch.

On his release, he went straight to the infirmary and heard that she'd kept mum all the while – Sidney was her last asset, too, when it came to that. But in return for her silence, he was to remove her from that dreadful place, and see to it she was well housed and well fed for the rest of her natural. Mrs Fox's partiality to 'living soft' is one of the few things directly attributed to her.

They did a deal. As she never wanted to be a charity case

again, Mrs Fox agreed to having the sort of life insurance taken out on her that would cover accidents as well as death, in the event of which, the big pay-out would go to Sidney – hence the will. Once that was done, they never stopped travelling.

There were two reasons for this. Hotel fraud was the easiest way of meeting his mother's demands, but it was essential that these hotels should be set well apart. And then there was the reason suggested by Sir Henry: Fox may have hoped that Fate would take a hand in tipping the teetering old woman off a train or – when that didn't seem so easy – a cross-Channel boat. He wouldn't have been the first person to baulk at murder while consciously increasing the odds of an Act of God. (Killing her in France should have been a cinch, only she wasn't insured while they were at Arras.)

They had been on the road for eight months by the time they arrived at the Hotel Metropole. It is possible that Mrs Fox was now very tired, and very fed-up with never being anywhere for more than two or three days. Her stamina, for a sufferer of Parkinson's disease, was more than remarkable, and one cannot help feeling somewhat sorry for her.

Fox kept telling the management they were off the following day, and kept having to find excuses for not leaving. Mrs Fox was presumably putting her foot down; she may have just wanted a decent rest, or she may even have said she wasn't budging until he'd found her a permanent place to stay. In other words, there was going to be no more travelling.

And no more travelling meant no more cheap insurance, and that knocked the carrot off the stick.

On the Sunday probably one of two things happened: either Mrs Fox started playing up and demanding to see a doctor – knowing Fox couldn't pay him – or he had her feign a chill to explain their continued residence. The evidence of other hotel managers indicates that he'd never before made such a mess of an illicit stay.

Then again, Mrs Fox may have really been ill – although Dr Austin didn't think so.

But it does seem to have been a turning point, however one reads it. Fox had come to the end of his pawnable possessions, and to the end of his patience. Fate was going to have to accept a little help on the next train journey he and his mother made.

That evening he told the barmaid about the dangerous prescription – just why, remains obscure. The Crown made a half-hearted attempt to hint heavily about overdoses, but Fox knew perfectly well that 'visible, external and violent means' were necessary for the policy's definition of accidental death. It would seem he was just trying to discredit Dr Austin in case the physician had been putting it about there was nothing the matter with old Mrs Fox.

What he did next morning was the significant thing. He used the prescription to get him enough money for the trip to London, and there he extended the policy until midnight on Wednesday. Now if Mrs Fox were to fall from a moving train well before then, then he had shown – by anticipating her existence on Wednesday night – just how unexpected her tragic death was. Conjurors use the same ploy when they concentrate their audience's attention on their most 'suspicious' hand, while the other hand does the trick.

That done, he returned to the Metropole late on Tuesday night and had words with his mother. They were moving out first thing in the morning, whether she liked it or not. Or perhaps he made up some story of a flat in London which she didn't believe. The exchange – whatever it was – led to such a violent reaction in her that Fox was forced to restrain her, and she tried to fight back. Her teeth, which she seldom wore except when eating, ended up on the carpet, and she bolted her door against him for the rest of the night.

Mrs Fox knew Sidney of old. There may have been something too eager about his insistence they left in the morning, something that warned her he was no longer to be trusted, however attentive to her he was the next day. She stayed put.

And he realized that only by humouring her was he going to get his mother away from the Metropole. To block any unexpected remark she might make about being man-handled, he told the barmaid and Miss Hopper about their 'sham fight', and then brought her down to dinner.

An hour or so later, he borrowed a paper for her and bought her half a bottle of her favourite tipple, which he shared with her in Room 66. There is nothing in the medical evidence to say when exactly Mrs Fox died – only that it could have been up to two hours before she was seen by Dr Austin – and this is when it could, in fact, have happened.

Text books on forensic medicine all have their examples of accidental strangling, which is usually the result of a rash action on the part of someone unduly provoked. They grab for their tormentor's throat and the next thing they know they have a corpse on their hands.

Fox was asked by Mr Cassels if he knew that one could throttle someone and not leave a mark. Like most laymen, he answered no, he did not. And so, when Mrs Fox collapsed back on her bed, he must have presumed she'd died of heart failure or shock.

This needed thinking about. He picked up the pillow, which had been knocked to the floor, and placed it absently on the pedestal. The teeth had only one proper place and that was in the washbasin. Then he went downstairs for a drink – not too much, he had to keep a clear head – and a careful assessment of his position.

When the lower bar closed, there was nothing for it but to go up to the room again. On the way there he saw Mr Harding looking at him in that unsettling way again, and it caught him right off balance. Still, he hadn't said anything.

Not a mark. Perhaps this was worth trying to cash in on. A little variation on that Lady Paget idea and . . . but he'd have to act quickly: it was now or never with three thousand pounds at stake. And why not – *he* hadn't really done anything, so what could they prove if it came unstuck?

Too late the caution from Mr Belloc's *Moral Alphabet*:

Learn from this justly irritating Youth,
To brush your Hair and Teeth and tell the Truth

Fox went on to make a comfortless sort of history by being the first murderer not to petition the Court of Criminal Appeal since its foundation. This may have been an admission of nothing but defeat.

And Captain Morse was successful in his divorce action, citing as co-respondent Cupid in the death cell.

Just another sick joke among so many . . .

Fox, the homosexual who solicited help in his vest, who chose an undertaker called Gore, who bought his mother a bunch of grapes as a prop, who told everyone they were heading for a dream-house known as 'End View'.

But perhaps the sickest joke of all was the one thing that

Dr Nichol did find in that handbag – which he'd been asked to search by a man whose name wasn't really Fox.

When Sidney Harry was hanged on the morning of April 8, 1930, the chances are that the good doctor saw it again in his mind's eye: a blank. black-edged mourning card, slightly scorched.

Chapter Three

THE BLAZING CAR MURDER

REX *v.* ALFRED ARTHUR ROUSE

JANUARY, 1931

A grotesque male form lay sprawled in the Northamptonshire village of Hardingstone that clear and frosty night. The moon was bright. It showed the limbs to be comically contorted, bent at impossible angles beneath the sacklike torso, and it picked out the amusingly bland stare of the long-lashed, unblinking eyes. Then a match was struck and applied to the carefully prepared pyre. In seconds the flames were jumping high, powdering into brief swirls of orange sparks at the tip, and within their pretty light, the pale face began to darken. Very soon, the heat was intense. The face altered shape, becoming fixed in a hilarious grimace before being charred to ash. While smoke, thick as cream, dribbled from the neck and sleeves of the cast-off jacket until the clothing, too, caught fire. An arm jerked back and crackled. A foot – burned through above the ankle – dropped off. But what really delighted the children of the village was the moment when the head exploded.

It was the Fifth of November, 1930. All over England effigies of Guy Fawkes were being burned on bonfires, and most of them had a charge of squibs under their battered trilby hats. In theory, the tradition commemorated the execution of a would-be assassin: in practice, it was just an excuse for a bit of ghoulish fun, as ephemeral as the fireworks themselves, and soon forgotten.

There occurred, however, a second blaze at Hardingstone that night which made all the others seem not so much a re-enactment, as some kind of ghastly dress-rehearsal. People everywhere were forced to recall vividly what they themselves had seen and done and heard. And, as detail matched detail from their own experience, an understandable if morbid fascination grew.

This second blaze was spotted at about 1.45 a.m. by two young villagers, Alfred Brown and his cousin William Bailey, who were strolling home after a Bonfire Night dance held in nearby Northampton. Just as they turned left off the main

London road, and started along Hardingstone Lane, two things caught their eye.

There was a very curious 'glare' around a bend some 600 yards ahead of them.

There was also a respectably-dressed man, wearing a light mackintosh and carrying an attaché case, apparently coming out of the ditch only a few paces away. They were struck by his being bareheaded.

In that moment the glare brightened.

'What's the blaze up there?' a puzzled Bailey asked Brown, as they hurried past the approaching stranger.

They had gone roughly 20 yards when the man shouted out behind them: 'It looks as if somebody has got a bonfire up there.'

This made them turn and look at him again. As Brown said later: 'A man – not being spoken to – answering us like that, it did seem strange.' They saw he was dithering at the road junction; he made a move in the direction of Northampton, another the opposite way towards London, and then stopped where he was.

All this had happened in under thirty seconds, giving them no opportunity to reflect. As soon as they saw the man pause, ending the momentary distraction, the cousins set off again – at a run.

Within 160 yards of the village they came on a car which was engulfed in flames fifteen feet high. There was nothing they could do, so Bailey sprinted to fetch his father, the village constable, while Brown went to alert PC Harry Copping, another policeman stationed at Hardingstone.

By the time all four men were at the fire, the flames had subsided somewhat and they were able to draw in close enough to see something like a football in the wreckage. Then, when a torch was brought to bear, it became plain that the 'ball' was, in fact, the head of a body sprawled across the remains of the two front seats.

PC Copping immediately sent his colleague to call the duty inspector, and then organized putting out the fire with buckets of water brought from the village. This took between ten and twelve minutes, and in the interim the head exploded with a dull sound.

Inspector James Lawrence and PC Robert Valentine arrived by car at 3.10 a.m. and the police began an examination of the scene.

Their first concern was the body.

It was on the passenger's seat, with its shattered head face-down on the driver's seat. The left arm couldn't be seen. The right arm extended upwards, ending in a burned-off stump at the elbow. The right leg, which had lost its foot, stuck out over the running board, while the left leg was doubled up so tightly under the torso that Inspector Lawrence was unable to conceive of how 'a human person could have got in that position'.

They decided that the remains were female; a theory which was lent further weight by PC Copping's find of a shrivelled-up leather heel, now of a size to suggest feminine delicacy.

Then there was the car to consider: a tiny Morris Minor, measuring a scant 3 ft. 4 ins. from door to door (the corpse was 3 ft. from crown to buttocks), and registered as MU 1468. The front half of the vehicle was superficially intact, although one tyre on the wire-spoked wheels had, like those at the rear, been destroyed by the fire. The bonnet was opened, and PC Valentine took the top off the petrol filler-pipe. The light from his torch showed the tank to be empty, nor could he find any sign of a rupture or leak.

This petrol tank was not itself in the engine compartment, but strapped to the other side of the bulkhead, in front of where the dashboard would ordinarily have been. From that point to the back bumper, the car was little more than a chassis and a pile of debris.

The only thing of any particular interest here – other than the body, of course – was a two-gallon petrol can in the ashes of the wood and lino flooring behind the driver's seat. The can had burst, and both its handle and screw cap were missing.

The actual position of the car was also studied. It had been parked about a foot from the grass verge, facing towards the main road and Northampton. The police used their head-lights to examine tyre marks left in the frost and loose gravel, and concluded that the Morris had been brought to a halt without any hard braking.

At about 4.45 a.m. it was decided to tidy up. Hardingstone Lane was a fairly busy road, being eighteen feet wide and part of five different bus routes, and dawn was approaching. The car was shifted over on to the grass verge, and then the body was taken to be locked in the garage of the Crown Inn at Hardingstone.

Where it looked, according to one official, 'more like a charred log of wood with burned branches attached'.

Such was the start of an investigation which was to prove in many ways as mystifying as the case itself.

There is, of course, no mystery attached to the casual behaviour of the police in Hardingstone Lane that morning, when not even a single note was taken. It remains, very simply, an object lesson in sheer unmitigated negligence. And it's ironic that they would later spend a day there, searching for a spot where someone claimed to have been caught with his pants down.

But it might be a mistake to similarly dismiss their even more perplexing behaviour still to come. After an early decision against involving Scotland Yard, they then went on to present the prosecution with a notably ragged pig's ear to turn into a silk purse – and yet nobody seems to have said anything about this. In fact, reading through what was written at the time, one senses very strongly that those 'in the know' are showing enormous restraint, and that there is, in fact, far more to the Blazing Car Murder than meets the eye.

Perhaps this is why the case has long been a favourite with armchair detectives, who may have noticed, too, that the police 'motive' is as obscure as that of the utterly astonishing man at the centre of it all. That a police motive must be 'good', whatever else it may be, only makes the matter all the more intriguing.

By retracing the story in detail, in much the same order as the facts emerged that winter, it is possible to understand the public's obsession to know more and more and more, even after it was too late for second thoughts.

This will also give everyone the same chance of tackling an infuriating but irresistible jigsaw puzzle. The image is trite, but the way the puzzle behaves isn't.

As millions discovered, when some of the pieces seem to fit, the picture won't make sense, and when part of the picture does make sense, not all the pieces lock together. To complicate things further, none of the edge pieces are included, and a niggling feeling develops that it should really cover a much larger area than indicated. Which is to say nothing of the curious blank pieces, like calculated blind spots, that keep cropping up.

For the next 36 hours or so, the Press had the major role to play in hastening events to a climax.

On the face of it, the routine police appeal, wired in to Fleet Street that morning by some provincial stringer, wasn't anything to get too excited about. Another car had burned out, which was a common enough occurrence in 1930, and a woman's body had been found in it. All the police were after was a possible witness to help them with 'forthcoming insurance inquiries' – a man aged 30–35, height 5 feet 10 inches to 6 feet with a small, round face, and curly dark hair. The appeal gave an idea of his clothing, and added he had no hat.

Now there was a thing: no hat? Being abroad without any headgear in the thirties tended to suggest, at the very least, circumstances most irregular. As J. C. Cannell of the *Daily Sketch* later observed, the hatless man made the appeal into a 'first-class mystery story'.

Evening papers all over Britain found a hole for a brief agency report in their early editions, even if it was tucked away in between Sinclair Lewis's Nobel Prize and the number of arrests for Guy Fawkes rags.

While in Fleet Street itself, the show got on the road. 'Ace' crime reporters were then in their heyday, and regarded themselves as investigators in their own right, if not as ancillaries of Scotland Yard. They seem to have put two and two together comparatively quickly.

A simple check showed that the Morris Minor MU 1468 belonged to a Mr Alfred Arthur Rouse, of 14 Buxted Road, London N12.

Two plain-clothes officers of the Metropolitan police called at this address early that afternoon. There they 'broke the news of the tragedy' to Mrs Lily May Rouse, who was under the impression her husband had called back to the house at 1 a.m. that day. She was asked to go directly to Northampton.

The crime reporters were at 14 Buxted Road too.

Before leaving, Mrs Rouse told the *Daily Express*: 'I have had many conflicting messages. I do not know whether it is my husband who is dead in the car or not.'

Mrs Rouse never gave evidence, and her statements to the

police were kept secret, but in an interview, published four months later, she said she'd been shown some clothing taken from the debris. It had meant nothing to her.

Mrs Rouse wasn't shown the charred body.

The local pathologist didn't see it himself until after seven that evening, when he began the first of three post-mortems held in the inn garage at Hardingstone.

Dr Eric Hemingway Shaw found it extremely difficult 'to form a definite and trustworthy opinion of a corpse which had been wrapped up in sacking and bundled about'. He did, however, manage to establish the cause of death: shock, resulting from burns – and appears to have thought it obvious that the remains were those of a grown man.

In fairness to the police, who had spent the morning scouring Northampton for news of a missing woman, it must be made clear that the genitals had been burned off. Yet so had the chest wall been burned off, which didn't leave much scope for assumptions about a hairless cadaver that was already missing such substantial parts as its hands and feet.

The dead man, said Dr Shaw, had been about 5 ft. 8 ins. tall, and – to judge by his teeth – in his early thirties. A description which rang a bell, and an odd one at that.

The police appeal had already become a main lead, eclipsing the just-discovered murder of Samuel H. Smith in Hull. By then the sub-editors must have known that between the lines lay the beginning of a sensational real-life serial; that they never gave an item more space than it warranted in their terms, is evident from this one-liner of the same day: 'Struck on the head by a machine in a hay field at Marlow, William Dean died.'

The *Daily Sketch* of November 7 had a photograph of the burned-out Morris on its all-pictures front page, and a lead heading on its main news page which read:

RIDDLE OF BODY FOUND IN BLAZING CAR
Police Inquiry for Hatless Passer By

Beneath this was a head-and-shoulders of Alfred Brown to go with his eye-witness account, the police appeal, and Mr Rouse's occupation – 'a traveller for a firm dealing in women's costumes.'

Messrs W. B. Martin and Co. dealt in men's braces, garters

and mackintoshes, and so this trifling inaccuracy is in itself informative: someone who knew that traveller, if only by repute, had been letting slip a few sly hints.

When an early edition of the *Daily Sketch* was delivered around breakfast-time to Primrose Villa, in Gellygaer, Glamorganshire, its effect upon the household was catastrophic – and led to the sudden departure of a guest.

All that remained then was for a Cardiff journalist to contact the police. He had been told of a lift to the coach station given to a Mr A. A. Rouse, whose initials had been on an attaché case, and who had made certain unsatisfactory remarks about the loss of a car.

Two thousand applied for the sixty seats available when the murder trial of Alfred Arthur Rouse, 36, opened in the seventeenth-century County Hall at Northampton on Monday, January 26, 1931.

A great deal had happened over the past eleven weeks to excite curiosity to an unusual degree.

One reason for this was the fact that the 'victim' hadn't been identified, and hundreds had sorrowfully claimed him for their own. The Great Depression had forced many men to leave home in the hope of finding work elsewhere, and frequently the shame of repeated failure kept them out of touch.

But the really tantalizing questions had arisen out of the police court proceedings which had, at first, seemed so straightforward.

There Mr G. R. Paling, for the prosecution, had said: 'He was a married man who was paying court to more than one woman other than his wife, and it might well be that he would have a wish to disappear and so unburden himself of the liabilities pressing upon him.'

And Mr Paling had called two women, Helen Campbell and Nellie Tucker, to give evidence of having the accused's illegitimate children, and there had been a statement from a third, Ivy Muriel Jenkins.

This made a fair bit of sense – although it didn't explain why the first two had posed so gaily for front-page pictures captioned: 'Mystery women in Rouse case.'

What jarred was the evidence of an insurance underwriter, Mr D. G. Kennedy, who told the magistrates that a £1,000 policy, effective from July 18 that year, had been payable on the death of a passenger in MU 1468, or on the death of the owner/driver.

Presumably, the policy had been evidence of motive, yet it wasn't at all clear how this fitted in: a man who 'disappeared' by pretending that somebody else's body was his own, could hardly claim that £1,000 himself.

And, as if this poser hadn't been enough, uppermost in most minds was the puzzling and very juicy statement that the accused had made to Inspector Lawrence soon after reaching Angel Lane police station in Northampton on November 8. When told Mrs Rouse was there to see him, he remarked:

'She really is too good for me. I like a woman who will make a fuss of me. I don't remember my wife ever sitting on my knee, but otherwise she is a good wife. I am very friendly with several women, but it is an expensive game. I was on my way to Leicester when this happened [he claimed the fire must have been accidental], to hand in my slip on Thursday morning to draw some money from my firm. I was then going to Wales for the weekend. My harem takes me to several places and I am not at home a great deal, but my wife doesn't ask questions now. I am arranging to sell my house and furniture. I was then going to make an allowance for the wife. I think I should clear between £100 and £150 from the sale.'

The words HAREM and ROUSE had been splashed on almost every newspaper bill in the land on the day after Inspector Lawrence had delivered this 'notorious speech' in evidence; many believed it sealed Rouse's fate by branding him as a callously immoral man 'who richly deserved a hanging' on that score alone, and it certainly prejudiced any further hearing.

To the relief of those who wanted to know *why* Rouse had made what seemed such a crazy boast, that had also been the day – December 17 – upon which he'd been committed for trial at the Winter Assizes. With this had come the promise that all would soon be explained.

The 60 successful applicants in their ringside seats were, however, in for a shock.

Something of that shock was felt by the more astute even before the first words of that extraordinary trial were uttered. In glancing about them, they noticed the familiar faces of people who had no right to be in court – not if they were going to give evidence later.

Then Rouse, who was brought by car every day from Bedford, appeared in the dock to claim everyone's attention. He had complained bitterly before the police court at having been made to wear borrowed clothes, and had plainly taken some care over what he was now dressed in: a brown suit, striped tie, starched collar, spats and polished brown shoes.

He had thick, dark hair combed straight back from a broad forehead, and intelligent blue eyes beneath heavy brows. His mouth was small, and his jaw rounded and fleshy. That was one description of him. Others ranged through 'alert, average, stocky' to the emphatic 'extremely good-looking' and the ambiguous 'debonair'. 'Agreeable' is another adjective that might have been applied, to judge from any portrait other than the rather gross one favoured by semi-official biographers.

Journalists who had been at the police court noted that he seemed slightly older and heavier, having lost some of his complacency on remand. This wasn't altogether a bad thing from Rouse's point of view, because his counsel had been forced to caution him against frivolity on that occasion.

Everyone present must have been struck by what a marked contrast his attractive qualities made with those of the exceedingly plain Mrs Rouse, whose red hair and front teeth were her most noticeable features.

Red hair also singled out the senior counsel for the prosecution, Mr Norman Birkett KC, who once said: 'I have found that it has added to my success.' This draper's son, who'd first shown his gift for advocacy by selling more remnants than anyone to farmers' wives on market day, went on to become Lord Chief Justice. He was spare, pale and not to be underestimated for his kindly, fumbling manner; he stressed important points with a gold pencil, and had a habit of drawling: 'Yeah?'

The Clerk of Assize, Mr George Pleydell Bancroft, who came of a famous theatrical family and was a playwright himself, knew Birkett well, having given him one of his first briefs. Just as he'd done for Mr D. L. Finnemore, the senior counsel for the defence, and so it was something of a reunion. Especially as Birkett had run a Boys' Brigade company for Finnemore during the war, and they'd shared chambers together at the start.

There was a hush as Mr Justice Talbot entered.

Rouse pleaded 'not guilty', the defence challenged two women jurors for obvious reasons, and Birkett rose to open the case for the Crown.

He told the jury that they needn't bother themselves about the victim having remained unidentified, as this made no difference to the law. Although, he added, they might find it a very significant factor.

Several onlookers registered mild surprise, but they hadn't heard anything yet.

The usual outline followed. Mr Birkett said the evidence would show that Rouse had murdered the unknown man, possibly after first stunning him with a mallet, by deliberately setting fire to his own car. And having turned the car into an inferno, Rouse had fled to a remote village in Wales, lying to everyone he met on the way.

The jury were told that as murder wasn't often committed in front of witnesses, circumstantial evidence had to be brought. But this was sometimes superior to direct evidence, and the prosecution believed that the logic of the circumstances and the facts of the case would lead them to only one conclusion.

Then came the shock.

Almost at the end of his speech, Mr Birkett said that it wasn't any part of the prosecution's duty to supply them with a satisfying or adequate motive for the crime. In fact, it didn't have to supply them with any motive at all – and wasn't going to.

Although, he again added, they might choose to think that Rouse had intended the charred body to be mistaken for his own, and that his plan had miscarried.

Now Sir Henry Curtis-Bennett had made the very same points about evidence and motive at the end of the Fox trial, but that hadn't missed out a great chunk of committal proceedings which had everyone on tenterhooks . . .

This dramatic change in prosecution tactics is said to have had a lot to do with the doubtful admissability of the testimony given by the 'mystery' women. Whatever the lower court had decided, the dictum was that nothing might be given in evidence which did not tend *directly* to the proof (or misproof) of matters at issue. And presumably Birkett wasn't taking any chances with the material he'd been handed.

From the defence point of view, this robbed them of an opportunity to score off inadmissability, and left them facing an opponent who'd exchanged a quiver of dodgy arrows for a pebble and a sling.

Which was none too comforting when one was hoping to create a giant doubt in the minds of the jury.

The Crown's evidence, however, got off to an embarrassing start that dominated the whole of the day.

Usually the formal identification of exhibits allows the court to settle down and arrange its papers and pencils. But the unfortunate Mr A. V. Ashford was soon being taken to task by the defence for having moved the steering wheel of the car 'to make a more effective photograph'.

It then turned out that the exhibits weren't official photographs in any sense of the term, and that Mr Ashford, an enterprising Northampton chemist, had taken them to sell to the Press.

'As I have already said,' Mr Ashford pointed out, much aggrieved, 'when I was taking photographs there were no police officers present, but there were members of the public there, over whom I had no control.'

Thus it was established that the roadside evidence had been left entirely at the mercy of passersby or, indeed, anyone else who might be tempted to tamper with it – and Mr Justice Talbot remarked upon this without amusement.

Soon afterwards the case-repairer, Mr Alfred Brown, took the stand and recalled what he and his cousin had seen while returning from the dance.

'Had anybody passed you on the road as you came up from Northampton before you got to the corner?' asked Mr Birkett.

'No, but just before we got to the corner, a little car passed us.'

And when it came to Mr William Bailey's turn, he also remembered the car passing them.

Mr Donald Finnemore, a tall, heavily-built man, who spoke in a slow, full-toned voice, and whose thoroughness, some said, verged on the laborious, asked if Rouse's shouted remark about a bonfire had surprised him.

'Yes.'

'And apart from what he shouted, the way he shouted struck

you as strange?'

'Yes, it did.'

'I don't know whether you can tell us this: did he sound hysterical?' Mr Finnemore went on, mindful of his client's claim to having been in a state of panic.

'I thought so at the time,' agreed Mr Bailey, 'but since hearing his voice, I think it was his natural voice.'

In fact, everyone who came across Rouse seems to have remembered this characteristic above all others. Mr Cannell said he'd never heard anything quite like it before; the pitch was very high, just short of a squeak – while another observer described it as 'a peculiar, female-like voice'.

Then PC Harry Copping took the oath and admitted to having taken no notes, and to having forgotten this and that.

PC Robert Valentine was the next policeman to be called. He gave very much the same evidence about the body's position, except that he was more precise about the right leg, explaining that it had protruded about eight inches over where the running board should have been.

The jury must have been impressed by this young man, who gave his evidence with confidence, and whose examination of the scene suggested an intelligent attempt to find reasons for the fire.

And he was the one police officer who said in court: 'Well, I thought it was important – a body being found in the car.'

But Sergeant Joe Harris, who'd discovered a mallet with hair on it around lunch-time on November 6, some 14 yards from the nose of the car, had a rather different impression to make.

'Of course, previous to your getting there,' said Mr Finnemore, 'a good many people would pass along that road going to work from Hardingstone?'

'Yes, I should think they would,' Sergeant Harris conceded, before raising eyebrows with: 'When I got there the car had not been moved. It was still standing in the road by the grass verge. I am confident about that.'

'Other officers say they moved it about four o'clock in the morning.'

'No,' came the reply. 'The marks on the road indicated that it was actually on the same spot where it burned, on my arrival.'

'When you got there it was still in the roadway?'

'Yes.'

'And not on the grass verge?'

'No, and indeed afterwards I assisted in moving it on to the grass verge. That would be about eleven o'clock. Superintendent Brumby, Constable Valentine and Inspector Lawrence assisted me in moving the car.'

Here was a prosecution witness alleging that other prosecution witnesses – all of them policemen – could (at best) be mistaken about when such a major undertaking had occurred.

But Mr Ashford's photographs showed the car on the verge at 8.15 that morning, and Mr Birkett made him look at one in an attempt to recover the situation.

Sergeant Harris stuck to his guns, whatever Exhibit 4 might conceivably prove, and said: 'That is my present state of mind.'

And on this note, the first day of the trial ended.

On Tuesday morning, Mrs Rouse was seen to powder her nose before the judge made his entrance.

Then Mr R. W. Tate, assistant surveyor to the county council, was recalled to produce a new map to be included among the exhibits. This may have seemed a dull start to the proceedings, but his evidence was to prove among the most damaging.

Oddly enough, what most people would remember best was a part of the defence's cross-examination.

'When one gets to that corner where the accused appears to have turned right to go through the village of Hardingstone,' Mr Finnemore asked him, 'would you see the lights of Northampton?'

'Yes, you would,' confirmed Mr Tate.

The highway leading to Northampton was a main road, and at the corner mentioned the only signpost said: *To Hardingstone*.

The next witness was Inspector James Lawrence, whose description of the body's position – a vital factor – differed slightly with regard to the right arm. Copping and Valentine had thought it looked as though it'd been stretched over the back of the passenger's seat. He remembered it extending upwards and backwards against this seat (which wasn't actually there any longer) in a far less natural position.

And in his opinion, the passenger had not been attempting

to escape from the car.

'At that time, I think, there was no thought in your mind that there might be a murder charge involved?' asked Mr Finnemore.

'Well, that is so. There were certainly some suspicious circumstances.'

'But you did not think it important or necessary – do not think I am making a complaint – to make, as soon as you could afterwards, an exact note of what you had seen?'

'Well, I did not do so.'

Inspector Lawrence also described his first encounter with Rouse, which had taken place at about one a.m. on November 8 at Hammersmith police station, after the accused had been detained on a coach by Detective-Sergeant Robert Skelly of the 'Met'.

Rouse had been cautioned and then asked if he would care to make a statement about the burned-out Morris. The statement had taken Sergeant Skelly four hours to write down, and then Rouse had been taken back to Northampton.

'The whole of the proceedings,' said Mr Finnemore, 'during which the statement was taken, occupied from one o'clock until about six in the morning?'

'No, just after five. There were, I think, four officers present – myself, Superintendent Brumby, and two London officers. During the taking of his statement the accused was asked a good many questions.'

'Did he appear to you to be giving a full and frank statement, and anxious to give it?'

'Well, he certainly made the statement,' answered Inspector Lawrence, 'but he did not appear to me to be telling the truth.'

This impression was based on Rouse's manner, he explained. The accused would say about a dozen words for the record, correct them three or four times, and then, while they were being written down, talk to the officers about something else.

'There was no need, in my opinion, if he was telling the truth, to correct anything,' said Inspector Lawrence.

'I suppose you never make mistakes?' Mr Finnemore remarked.

'I suppose I have done so, like other people.'

A question later, Mr Finnemore said: 'Have you ever found it difficult to recall events you have been asked about?'

'At times, yes.'

Inspector Lawrence agreed that he knew Rouse had a war wound in the head which was said to make him excitable and that he'd claimed to have panicked in Hardingstone Lane, but this made no difference to the impression the man was lying.

Asked to give an example of how Rouse had changed parts of his statement, he said that the accused had first stated he hadn't called out to Brown and Bailey 'Then he corrected it by saying that he saw in the paper he was reported to have said that. He then said that he was not sure whether he had said it or not, and, therefore, he did not want it recorded.'

An automobile engineer Mr W. E. B. Dickens, then made a brief appearance to say that the car had been left in second gear.

His place in the box was taken by Colonel Cuthbert Buckle, a spruce but not particularly military-looking man – his photograph in the papers that morning reminds one faintly of Frank Sinatra.

'I am a full-pay colonel in the British Army in command of a territorial brigade,' he said, 'and I am a Commander of the Order of the British Empire and a Companion of the Noble Order of the Bath. I have had twenty-six years' experience as a fire assessor, and during that time I have had experience with regard to fires of all kinds, numbering upwards of ten thousand.'

No jury could have failed to respond attentively to that introduction.

Colonel Buckle was to spend more time giving evidence than anyone else at the trial, with the exception of Rouse himself. To appreciate the main inferences he drew, it is perhaps simplest to begin by considering a basic principle involved.

If an explosion is to be avoided, one must ignite petrol before it becomes admixed with air. Anyone hoping to burn a body beyond recognition would want to take such a precaution or else the body might be blown clear – and land relatively intact. Moreover, they'd need a fire that burned at a tremendously high temperature for at least several minutes, because a body is chiefly water and doesn't reduce to ash very readily.

After Colonel Buckle had said he'd never before seen a lower radiator water joint burned out in a roadside fire, Mr

Birkett asked him:

'Does that give you an impression of the intensity or nature of the fire?'

'Yes. There was an unusually intense fire under that bonnet, and it was a continuous fire which was fed for a period of time.'

Colonel Buckle was sure this fire had started in the body of the car, and referred to the state of the brass windscreen frame.

'Brass fuses at 1,850 degrees Fahrenheit,' he told the court. 'Upon examination of the windscreen frame, I found it to be cut through as if by a blow-pipe flame at the bottom. The top is cut through more or less vertically over the same place, and nearly cut through here.'

This had brought his attention to the nut around the tap on the main fuel line leading from the bottom of the tank immediately below the cut marks. This nut, he discovered, was one whole turn loose. So he had gone over to a police car, which had the same fuel system, and tried an experiment. By slackening the nut three-quarters of a turn, he found the petrol leaking out quite freely, and in 80 seconds it had filled a half-pint tumbler to the brim.

Mr Birkett asked what would happen if the tank were subjected to heat.

'You would get pressure in the tank, and instead of being a flow at ordinary pressure, it is a flow at extraordinary pressure, and it comes out at several times the rate.'

There was an eerie reminder of Guy Fawkes Night in Colonel Buckle's further description of what sort of fire had been involved: 'You get a very curious flame structure. You get a roaring flame which forcibly feeds itself with air and whistles and roars. Such flames are very pretty; they are like an ostrich feather – they have curls all round the outside edge of them.'

He added that these flames must have come from a more or less vertical stream of petrol escaping from the loose union below the windscreen.

'If these joints did come loose, you would have cars blowing up in the streets,' he said in reply to a question from the judge.

'And the manufacturers of them would disappear, I should imagine?'

'And the drivers and owners, m'lord,' said Colonel Buckle.

Mr Finnemore was interested to know why the petrol can had been virtually dismissed, and made this one of the first points in his cross-examination.

'The flames always go up,' explained Colonel Buckle. 'I mean things were burned at the bottom. A petrol can does not go off with a big explosion. Supposing the can was standing up as it is now, I should expect it to fall down. It would not go up with the pressure of that burst (in the side).'

Besides which, any fire started by the petrol can wouldn't last long.

Mr Finnemore had it verified that it was petrol vapour rather than the liquid which ignited, and then asked: 'When you get a fire of that sort in a motor car, the flame is all over the car almost instantaneously, is it not?'

'Yes.'

'Do I understand you say it is like feeding a bonfire?' Mr Justice Talbot interjected. 'You may not have a great blaze at the start, which may be caused in the way put to you, but what you find here is the intense flame going on for a considerable time, and so strong that it will fuse metal?'

Colonel Buckle agreed this was so.

He also had to agree with Mr Finnemore that there was nothing whatsoever to indicate with any certainty how the primary fire had been started.

But they clashed over the blaze under the bonnet, and Rouse, who always took a keen interest in what expert witnesses had to say, leaned forward.

'Where does that fire come from?' Mr Finnemore asked.

'From the burning petrol.'

'The whole case is that the fire starts in the body of the car, is it not? That is the case which you have been putting all the time?'

'Yes, but it may have also started under the engine. There has been a fire there, but when that started, I do not know.'

'Is not the obvious explanation this: that the carburettor, while still full of petrol, bursts, and that sprays petrol on the engine and causes the fire there?'

'I do not think so.'

'Is it not the only reasonable explanation?' demanded Mr Finnemore.

'I do not agree,' said Colonel Buckle.

Although he had to admit there was no evidence of there being a fire under the carburettor before it either burst or melted – or even, in Mr Finnemore's own words – that something happened to the carburettor itself.

The colonel's next clash was with the judge, having begun a reply: 'May I remind you of the evidence – '

'Never mind about me,' cut in Mr Justice Talbot, 'but with people like you expert gentlemen, you think a lot of things are understood which are not understood, and what counsel is trying to do is get the impression produced that your view is favourable to his case. That is what he is here for. What I want to know is why you say that the tank must have been either full or very nearly full?'

Rebuked but undaunted, Colonel Buckle answered with an edge: 'Because of the remarkable *evidences* in various places of relatively long continuous fire, which I stressed in my examination-in-chief.'

Mr Finnemore was able to win two useful admissions from him before sitting down again. One was that it was just possible for a passenger to touch the fuel tap with his toecap, and the other was that the nut could be loosened by vibration – however unlikely the idea appeared.

During his re-examination, Mr Birkett had Colonel Buckle explain why it was equally unlikely the top of the carburettor had been blown off, and flatly refute the defence suggestion that the can 'might have gone off like a bomb'.

'Again, supposing there had been a leakage from the petrol can, either from the brass screw or on the surface, what would you have expected to find if there was the striking of a match by a "foolish man" upon it [another defence suggestion], and the petrol on the can was ignited?'

'Just flashes of flame.'

Mr Birkett added a finishing touch: 'Would it be such a fire as that from which escape would be easy?'

'Yes,' Colonel Buckle said with a nod.

All the while he had been keeping a careful watch on the prisoner. On finally leaving the witness box, he confided: 'There is some explanation of the fire which Rouse is expecting me to give which I have not discovered.'

And he went away to think about it. Someone sitting near the dock had also noticed something, although they apparently didn't disclose this until later: every time a certain part of the car had been mentioned, Rouse had stiffened the muscles of one leg.

The last witness of the day had quite a bit to say about the stiffening effect which heat can have on legs.

It was, in fact, the basis of an astounding discovery made by Dr E. H. Shaw, the Northampton pathologist, during his second post-mortem on the body on November 8 (a third took place on November 10, attended by Sir Bernard Spilsbury).

Dr Shaw described the find after telling the court of his regret at not having seen the body *in situ*, and that he hadn't been able to form any conclusion from the posture owing to it being manhandled.

'I follow that,' said Mr Richard Elwes for the Crown, 'but supposing the left knee had been drawn up as far as it could be drawn up, do you think that could be explained by the heat of the fire?'

Heat flexion must have been intense, agreed Dr Shaw – 'because in my examination I have found petrol-soaked clothing in between the leg and body.'

He added that the strips of cloth were still damp when he removed them.

The left leg had been pressed back so hard that the fire had no way of reaching the petrol in the fabric – nor even of evaporating it. A fire which, as Colonel Buckle had proved, must have been burning at over 1,800 degrees Fahrenheit, within inches of the body.

Then Dr Shaw turned to the question of the hairs on the mallet picked up by Sergeant Harris. The most he could say about them was that one was probably a fragment of human hair of a lightish colour.

Under cross-examination by Mr Finnemore, Dr Shaw also said: 'I examined the mallet to see if there were any signs of blood or bloodstains upon it, but there were none. There was no skin or tissue or anything of that sort.'

And the court was adjourned.

That night Colonel Buckle reviewed his chain of reasoning, but Wednesday was to bring an end to expert evidence for the time being, once Sir Bernard Spilsbury had added his own observations to those of Dr Shaw. From here on, the 'human issue' would dominate, confuse and enliven the proceedings, leaving the jury to base their decision on what they realized was only a very small part of the whole story – if that.

The Home Office Pathologist began by confirming Dr Shaw's findings, and then explained that, from the carbon deposits in the air passages, and from the amount of carbon monoxide in the blood, he had deduced the man had died within half a minute of the fire starting.

The Crown needed the weight of his words to crush any notion that the man had been the victim of an accident.

So Mr Birkett said: 'My learned friend, Mr Finnemore, suggested to Inspector Lawrence that possibly the position of the body was consistent with a violent attempt to get across to the off-side to get out of the car. What do you your-self say with regard to that position in the Morris Minor saloon?'

'I think it is consistent with the man either pitching forward,' replied Sir Bernard, 'or being thrown down, face down-wards, on the seats of the car from the near-side door.'

The position of the legs was the next thing to have settled.

'What would be the effect of intense heat on the limbs?'

'After the man had died, the heat in this case would be so intense as to spread rapidly through the skin to the muscles, and would progressively overheat them, and produce the condition of what is known as heat stiffening or heat rigor.'

'What would be the effect of heat rigor upon the muscles of the left leg?'

'It would forcibly shorten and contract the muscles, and would cause the limb to be bent. The leg would be bent upon the thigh, and the thigh would be bent upwards over the abdomen.'

Sir Bernard said he'd seen the clothing found by Dr Shaw, and that there'd still been a smell of petrol present on November 10.

'What do you say,' Mr Birkett asked him, 'about the pro-jection of the right leg beyond where the door was, according to the evidence in the case?'

'I think that clearly shows that the door must have been open, and that no doubt both legs were extended in the same way originally.'

In his opinion, the petrol found in the scraps of clothing had been either distributed at that level during the early part of the fire, or it had soaked in before the fire started.

He couldn't add to what Dr Shaw had said about the hairs on the mallet.

Mr Finnemore reminded the jury that the man had died from shock after the blaze had begun, and he then said: 'On the body itself, I take it, there was no sign of any injury caused during life?'

'No.'

'We heard from Dr Shaw that the vault of the skull had been broken in a number of places?'

'Yes. That was due to bursting and splintering through the effects of the heat, obviously.'

'In addition to there being no sign of any injury caused during life, I think also, apart from the carbon monoxide, there was no other poison at all in the body?'

'No; none that would produce obvious changes.'

Sir Bernard was, however, unable to agree that the man could have taken up such a position with the doors shut (there didn't seem room) *and*, after death, extend his right leg once the door had collapsed: it would have been pinned down by the body, and have contracted like the left one.

So much for the dead man. Now came the moment to learn more about the accused himself who was, as usual, taking a lively interest in things.

Mr J. B. Graham, the company secretary who saw to his salary, commission and expenses, said that Rouse received about £500 a year – which was a good income in those days. Sometimes Rouse was given commission in advance, although Mr Graham quaintly noted he hadn't asked for any more commission on account since November 4.

Miss Nellie Tucker, one of the women who had given evidence at the police court, was called – and then asked to withdraw. The jury were also asked to retire to their room.

When they came back again, all Miss Tucker said was this: 'I live at 49 Hendon Way, Hendon. I have known the accused, Mr Rouse, for nearly five years. I saw him last on the fifth of November. It was about 7.10 when I saw him, and about eight o'clock he left. It was in City Road, London, where I saw him.'

Her only statement under cross-examination amounted to:

'He was proposing to see me again the next week, on the Monday, the tenth.'

For many of those present, this must have been a little like hearing spring had been cancelled.

At 11.15 that same evening, said PC David Lilley, he'd come across the accused in a small saloon parked at the side of the road near Markyate, north of St Albans. Rouse had apologized after being told his rear light was out, and had switched it on again immediately.

'The accused was dressed in a light coat and trilby hat,' PC Lilley told the court. 'The man that was sitting on his left-hand side appeared to me to be about thirty-five to forty years of age. He was a man of small stature, had an oval, pale face, and was dressed in a dark coat and trilby hat.'

This evidence had dealt with the 'before' of the blaze, now it switched to the 'after', beginning at two a.m. when Mr Henry Herbert Turner, a London lorry driver, was stopped by a hatless man within sight of a fire at Hardingstone.

Rouse had said he'd missed a lift with a friend. The fire had not been mentioned; they had discussed cars, mechanical defects, and the journeys made by the accused, mainly in Wales. Rouse had worked the headlight switch from Markyate to London, where he had been dropped off at Tally Ho Corner around six. He seemed 'rather hurried' and went down Friern Barnet Road.

And at 8.30 that morning, Rouse appeared to be 'in a bit of a stew' to a coach company porter whose help he sought in London.

But the coach company manager, Mr Eric Farmer, had found the traveller in 'very good spirits' while a booking was being made for him to journey to Wales.

Rouse had explained that his car, a Wolseley Hornet, with a Stetson hat in it, had been stolen from outside a lorry driver's coffee stall. 'He appeared more worried about the loss of the hat than the loss of the car – I am quite clear about that,' said Mr Farmer.

The accused had dithered over whether to buy a single or return, asked how to reach Leicester from Wales without touching London, and made a 'jocular remark' about Black and White whisky. He finally took a single ticket on an express coach leaving at 9.15.

The driver of this coach was Mr George Bell, behind whom

Rouse chose to sit on the journey to Newport; they had talked together, and Rouse had remarked on the loss of his car outside a pull-up near St Albans.

'Further on in the journey, he told me that he was going down to Wales to see his wife,' said Mr Bell. 'As to where his wife was, that was a point he was rather uncertain about.'

They'd also talked about mallets, which they both used for knocking out dents, and about an accident Rouse had caused, through becoming sleepy, which had injured the other party.

There was a decided stir in the public gallery when Mr William Jenkins, a colliery proprietor, of Primrose Villa, Gellygaer, Glamorganshire, took the oath.

The whole front page of the *Daily Sketch* on December 10 had featured pictures of Rouse and his mysterious women friends, and by far the most attractive of them had been the demure Ivy Muriel Jenkins.

But Mr Jenkins was not there to explain anything, nor to provide more than the bare and impersonal facts. His daughter had gone to London as a probationer nurse, he said, and she had returned home with the accused. His daughter had been taken ill at the end of October.

'The accused came to my house from Thursday to Monday morning once a fortnight,' Mr Jenkins stated.

The accused's last visit had been in response to a telegram telling him that Ivy was very ill. After explaining that his car had been stolen in Northampton, he had gone up to see the patient.

Later on that evening, the accused had denied that a car described in a newspaper was his own. The next morning the *Daily Sketch* had repeated the car story and given the accused's name. The accused had gone away in a car driven by a business acquaintance.

In answer to a question by Mr Finnemore, the father recalled the accused having said he wanted to go back to London and report the loss of his car to the police.

Miss Phyllis Maud Jenkins, the sister of the ill girl, said that the accused hadn't mentioned his car to her on the evening of his arrival. The first she knew about it was when the *Daily Sketch* was delivered in the morning.

'I called him down, and told him there was a photograph

of his car in the paper. He asked me how I knew, and I said his name, "A. A. Rouse", was underneath. He then took the paper and looked at it. He went back upstairs with the paper. The next I saw of it was when my mother brought it down a few moments afterwards. The accused asked if he could keep the paper. I said "yes" and he took it away.'

Mr Finnemore did not cross-examine.

A collier, Mr Thomas Reakes, added a little colour with his description of Rouse's entrance that night – and inadvertently let slip more than he might have wished, seeing he was a friend of the family.

Mr Reakes said the accused's first sentence had been: 'Oh, dad, I have been a long time coming, about eighteen hours on the road.'

It was Mr Reakes who had returned to the house that night with an evening paper, having heard about the loss of the Morris near Northampton.

'I handed him the paper and said: "Is this your car? If it is you will see it no more." He looked at the paper and said: "That is not my car." '

Mr H. J. Brownhill, a motor salesman, said he'd been talking to Mr Jenkins about a business matter the following morning when Rouse had come out of the house in his shirt sleeves and asked for a lift back to Cardiff.

On the way back, Mr Brownhill had asked Rouse about his car, and was told it'd been stolen and then burned.

'When he told me he had reported it to the police and to the insurance company, I told him he had nothing to worry about.'

They had stopped at an hotel for a few minutes, and Rouse had walked out of the room when a butcher's boy spoke about there being the remains of a charred woman in the debris of his car.

Mr Brownhill said he had 'communicated with the police' later in the day.

The butcher's boy, Idwal Morris, expanded on Rouse's reaction to his mention of 'the charred remains of a lady'.

He told the court: 'The prisoner said: "Oh, dear, dear, I cannot bear to hear anything more about it," and he went out.'

With witness after witness now spending only a few minutes in the box, the increased tempo of the trial had everyone tensed for the conclusion of the Crown case.

A car salesman appeared to say he'd made a part-exchange on the Morris Minor MU 1468. A hire-purchase dealer gave Rouse's monthly repayment as £6 14s 8d, and added that all borrowers had to insure their vehicles.

The underwriter, Mr D. G. Kennedy, gave evidence once again about the £1,000 comprehensive policy, and said that Rouse had declared the car would be used 'solely for pleasure purposes'.

Among the comments Rouse had made on the proposal form, which Mr Kennedy read out, was: 'Do you wish to cover all accidents to passengers in addition to your legal liability?' – 'Never got any passengers, but yes.'

Then at last Detective-Sergeant Robert Skelly of the Metropolitan Police was called to give his account of that initial encounter Rouse had had with the law.

'At 9.20 on the seventh of November I went, with Detective Constable Holland, to a motor coach which was then standing in the Hammersmith Bridge Road.

'I saw the accused seated in the coach. I caused somebody else to ask him to alight. I then spoke to him. I said: "Are you Mr Rouse?" and he said, "Yes, that is right."

'I said: "We are police officers, and I want you to accompany me to the police station."

'He said: "Very well. I am glad it is over. I was going to Scotland Yard about it. I am responsible. I am very glad it is over. I have had no sleep." '

On their arrival at the police station, and even before sitting down, Rouse said in response to hearing the Northampton police wanted to interview him:

'I suppose they wish to see me about it. I do not know what happened exactly. I picked up the man on the Great North Road; he asked me for a lift. He seemed a respectable man, and said he was going to the Midlands. I gave him a lift; it was just this side of St Albans. He got in and I drove off, and after going some distance I lost my way. A policeman spoke to me about my lights.

'I did not know anything about the man, and I thought I saw his hand on my case which was in the back of the car.

'I later became sleepy and could hardly keep awake. The engine started to spit and I thought I was running out of petrol. I wanted to relieve myself, and said to the man: "There is some petrol in the can; you can empty it into the tank while I am gone," and lifted up the bonnet and showed him where to put it in. He said: "What about a smoke?" I said: "I have given you all my cigarettes as it is."

'I then went some distance along the road, and had just got my trousers down when I noticed a big flame from behind [*sic*]. I pulled my trousers up quickly and ran towards the car which was in flames. I saw the man inside, and I tried to open the door, but I could not, as the car was then a mass of flames. I then began to tremble violently. I was all of a shake.

'I did not know what to do, and I ran as hard as I could along the road where I saw the two men. I felt I was responsible for what had happened. I lost my head, and I didn't know what to do, and really don't know what I have done since.'

Rouse had then explained that he'd taken the attaché case with him because the passenger's hand had been on it.

'Was he being detained then as a person from whom a statement was wanted?' asked Mr Finnemore, with the intent of adding to the picture of his client's willing helpfulness.

'Well, that is very difficult for me to answer,' replied the Metropolitan policeman. 'I did not know what Northampton wanted to do with him. I only knew they wanted to see him, and that was why he was there. Up to the time when the Northampton police arrived, he was not cautioned or anything.'

Sergeant Skelly also commented on the fact Rouse was a very rapid speaker, and that he'd stuck to his story of an accidental fire all the way through.

Mr Birkett said in re-examination: 'During the time that statement was being given, what was his general demeanour?'

'To my mind he gave me the impression that he seemed very happy.'

And that was almost it – except for a couple of loose ends, one of which indirectly gave a most unexpected glimpse of Rouse's domestic life.

Mr Bowen Westbrooke, an advertising agent who had known Rouse for over two years, went into the box to say:

'I remember August of last year when I was camping with my family at Barton, near Luton, and the accused was also camping there with his wife and an adopted child.

'We slept in tents. The mallet, which is Exhibit No. 32, I have seen before. I know it belongs to the accused. He was using it at that time when we were in camp for knocking tent pegs in.'

He was using it *at that time* for tent pegs . . . how this does suggest a certain grim pedantry, or even humour.

There was certainly something mildly comic in the evidence of Superintendent G. W. Brumby which followed. It involved explaining that a special search had been made for some sign of where Rouse had allegedly 'eased himself' – the problem being that Superintendent Brumby couldn't think of a polite euphemism for the noun, and went off at a Rouse-like tangent before saying, despairingly: 'I mean that I went to look for what would have come from him.'

To no avail.

Superintendent Brumby also gave Rouse's reaction to being charged with murder on Saturday afternoon, November 8: 'I cautioned him, and he said: "I am quite innocent." '

And recalled that when the accused had seen the mallet at Angel Lane police station, he'd admitted at once: 'That is mine.'

Then, for anyone who had spared a thought for the apparently long-suffering proprietor of the Crown Inn, whose garage had been used as a mortuary for the best part of a week, Superintendent Brumby disclosed that the body was now in a sealed tank in Northampton. (Possibly, of course, having Sir Bernard Spilsbury attend a post-mortem on the premises was almost as good as being able to claim 'Queen Elizabeth slept here'.)

Mr Birkett rose to end on a sobering note.

'My Lord, there was the accused's statement. When before the justices, in response to the charge, he said:

' " I am quite innocent of this charge. I have given my statement. I am not a wealthy man, and, whether I am found guilty or not, my all is taken. I do not wish to give evidence: I do not wish to call witnesses."

'That is the case for the Crown.'

Only two people gave evidence on Thursday – one of them was Alfred Arthur Rouse.

But Mr Finnemore had first to complete his opening address to the jury on behalf of the defence. He reminded them that the law made their burden bearable by insisting the case had to be proved beyond all reasonable doubt.

And proceeded to show how, in his view, doubt riddled the prosecution's case, in which the facts were at least as consistent with innocence as with guilt, if not more so.

The story that the jury had been asked to believe was almost incredible, especially as the evidence hadn't provided a motive. Whatever the requirements of the law, motivation was still crucial in such a case. In what way had the accused tried to disappear? He'd gone to the very place where he was expected.

Alfred Arthur Rouse certainly did talk quickly. The court shorthand writers and reporters had difficulty in keeping up with him.

As for his actual demeanour in the witness box, upon which the Crown had hoped to rely fairly heavily, it was described as alternating between buoyant self-confidence and apparent candour, on the one hand, and an argumentative, defensive aggression on the other.

What particularly irked his listeners, among them some who were most sympathetic, was to hear a person under oath repeatedly use expressions like *honestly*, *candidly* and *to be quite frank*. The disenchanted said one couldn't believe any six words he said, and plainly the defence was discomfited by his eagerness to add words and be too explanatory.

It is important to note that few of these nuances were picked up by the newspaper-reading public, and this was to have its consequences.

During his evidence, Rouse made two replies that have been remembered down the years. The first was in answer to the tenth question put to him by Mr A. P. Marshall, his other counsel, and its effect on the jury was discernible.

'I joined up on the eighth of August, I think it was,' said Rouse, outlining his war service, 'and I was wounded on the fifteenth of April; I believe it was February. The twenty-fifth of May, 1915, I think it was.'

Right third time.

'I was wounded on the left part over my temple, at the left of the head,' Rouse went on, 'and my left leg just above the knee, and, of course, I was blown up at the time – I think it was just previous to that – and I think I had one or two small scratches previous. They were not really serious.'

Mr Marshall asked if the temple wound had affected him in any way.

'Previous to the war, I had no complaint or no one had any cause to complain of my memory; but most people seem to think now that my memory is somewhat erratic at times, and have told me so.'

He was then prompted to remember what he'd done on November the fifth.

Rouse had spent the day going round businesses south of London; at some stage or other – he couldn't recall exactly when – he'd filled up his petrol tank (or almost, he supposed), and had placed a petrol can in his car. That evening, at roughly nine o'clock, and after his wife had packed a case for him, he had left for Leicester. His intention had been to call at his firm's factory first thing in the morning, collect some samples, and, more importantly, some money he felt they owed him.

'From Leicester where did you intend to go?' said Mr Marshall.

'To Gellygaer, South Wales.'

Mr Marshall had him return to the events of Guy Fawkes Night.

The unknown man had asked for a lift near Tally Ho Corner and Rouse, pleased to have company, had agreed.

'I have an idea he was respectably dressed; a collar and tie he certainly had, and his clothes were quite in good repair and order,' he said, before going into rather dithery detail over the coat.

'He was about my own build, but not perhaps so meaty, perhaps not quite so stout; but about the same build otherwise.'

'Did you notice anything about his speech?'

'He was not a Londoner; he was an Englishman. Very likely he was a country man; he might have been from the south. He spoke with a country accent.'

It was becoming clearer all the time why Sergeant Skelly had had his problems writing down the statement, and why he had not been unduly disturbed by Rouse's habit of pulling thoughts together with a string of haphazard words.

An attempt to doze for a few minutes near St Albans had been cut short by a policeman remarking on the car's rear light being out. After that, they had continued north towards Northampton until Rouse realized he was going through a village he didn't recognize.

'I do not know the name of the road – is it Hardingstone Lane? – but I went to the turning on the left. I had gone some distance – I could not say how far I went along – when my companion suddenly said: "This would be a fine place" or "good place" or words to that effect, "for your sleep" or "doze".'

Rouse had stopped and decided that his passenger should earn his keep while he went off to relieve himself. The car had been spluttering, and he wanted his petrol tank topped up. First he had opened the offside of the bonnet to show the man where the filler pipe was situated; then he had taken the screw cap off the petrol can, and put it back on a thread or two. The can itself he'd placed on the driver's seat.

As he was leaving the car, he had tossed the man an unwanted cigar, in response to a plea for a smoke, and had checked to see if his 'down-and-out' passenger had a light for it.

Seeing the sudden glare, Rouse had stumbled back 250 yards or so, doing up his trousers.

'I ran towards the car, and when I got there I could not approach it,' he said – which wasn't quite what he had told Sergeant Skelly.

'Of course, I was a bit panic-stricken. I went as near the car as I could. I think one of the first thoughts I thought was: my car will explode; my petrol tank will explode. I know I ran past the car towards the village, I take it, for help – I do not remember exactly what my thoughts were. I know I said something, "My God, my God!"

'I did not know what to do. I turned round and ran back on the grass verge to see if I could do anything, presuming the man was inside. I did not know; I could not see him or anything. I got terrified of the sight, and ran.'

Rouse, who flushed under the stress of emotion, had been becoming redder all the time. Now he broke down and wept for nearly a minute; he was given a glass of water and allowed to sit.

The meeting with the two cousins followed – his first thought had been to get help from them.

'Whether I spoke to them or what I did I do not know. I got to the main road, and I suppose the next thought was to get help from a lorry – more efficient, because a man would not be much help in putting out a fire; you want an extinguisher, or something of that sort. I lost my head, and ran this way and that.'

Mr Marshall had him retrace the journey to the coach station and then asked: 'At that time did you think you ought to see the police first?'

'I do not think I was worrying so much,' said Rouse. 'I was worried about everything. I had made all my plans beforehand. Pardon me, what day was the sixth?'

A Thursday, he was told.

'I had made my plans for Thursday, Friday and Saturday, and I also wanted particularly to get back to London on the Monday,' Rouse explained, going on to say how the loss of his car had brought these plans to a standstill.

He added: 'Well, I had promised to go down to Wales, and I went.'

His counsel eventually brought the examination to a close by asking him if he'd done anything wrong at all in Hardingstone Lane that night.

'Nothing criminal at all,' said Rouse, although he had been very likely wrong in running away.

'Did that fact trouble you at all afterwards?'

'Yes, afterwards, it naturally did.'

Having attempted to demonstrate a degree of compassion in a man widely believed to be callous – those police court hearings haunted every moment of the defence's efforts, the final task was to do something about the aftermath and its negative aspects.

'You know that subsequently you told things which were not true,' said Mr Marshall. 'What do you say now about that? In South Wales, for example, you gave explanations which were not true?'

Rouse nodded and said: 'I gave the explanations which I thought were most suitable at the moment. I did not want to give a full explanation. As I say, there were ladies present each time, for one thing, and it was rather a long story, and I should never have got to the end of it, and I gave the nearest for the time being to let them know. They would know eventually in any case.'

Mr Marshall, who shared Mr Finnemore's absolute belief in the innocence of their client, for all his shortcomings, made this the last question before the Crown began its lengthy cross-examination:

126

'Do you know exactly just what happened that night?'

It was meant, of course, to strike home at the doubts of every single person in the courtroom.

'Not in the car; no,' replied Rouse.

The pale, shrewd face of Mr Norman Birkett turned towards him. The thin gold pencil case glinted. Snow fell outside and the air was chill.

'You think it was unfortunate that you should tell lies in Wales?'

'It turned out to be subsequently, now, perhaps against me.'

'What do you mean when you say that it has turned out against you?'

'People seem to think I did tell lies,' Rouse said, 'and I admit I did tell lies. My name has been clear up to now of lies.'

'Do you think an innocent man might have told the truth?'

'Yes, no doubt, to your way of thinking.'

'No, I merely want the fact.'

'I think I did the best possible thing under the circumstances.'

'Still, do you?'

'Yes.'

'Still?'

'If I had given a long explanation to them they would have kept on asking me questions about it, and it would have been very unpleasant for them.'

'Is it a fact,' asked Mr Birkett, 'that to all the people whom you saw, from two o'clock on the morning of the sixth to nine-thirty on the evening of the seventh, you never told a word of the truth to any one of them?'

'I do not know what you mean by a word of the truth. I had lost the car, and I intended to go down there.'

Rouse's ability to look after himself – as he would presumably have seen it – became clear when Mr Birkett asked him if he'd spent November 7 (the day of the *Daily Sketch* report) thinking of what explanation he would give the police.

'You are inferring that I tried to make up a story,' the prisoner told him. 'Is that it? Say "yes" and I will answer it.'

Mr Birkett did not say yes, but elicited a denial all the same.

If that had made anyone in the public gallery blink, then Rouse soon had them blinking again – and twice as hard. In fact, the irony of what he said seems to have totally distracted everyone, including Mr Birkett, from noticing that the remark might have had a certain significance at another level.

It was pointed out to him that he'd had abundant opportunities of 'getting it over with' before being met by Sergeant Skelly; twelve hours before, when catching the coach back to London, he had been within 41 yards of the Cardiff police station.

'If I had seen it, I should not have gone in,' said Rouse, then came the stunner: 'My reason is I have very little confidence in local police stations.'

There was a pause.

Mr Birkett did, however, return to this statement a little later on: 'But you would not have gone to the provincial police because you do not trust provincial police?'

'If you want my candid opinion, I have not much faith in them. I was going to the fountain-head [Scotland Yard]. One usually goes to the fountain-head if one wants things done properly.'

Insult reluctantly added to injury; or so it may have appeared to some of the officers present.

Rouse's admission of 'I am responsible', which he'd made to Sergeant Skelly in the street, needed further explanation, said Mr Birkett.

'Let us see what the degree of responsibility was.'

'Thinking it over, I will tell you. I handed the man a cigar. I asked him to fill up my car with petrol. I did not know whether he was capable of doing that, filling it with petrol.'

Then why had Rouse let him do it?

'Quite frankly, he volunteered himself; I think quite frankly he did; I am not certain.'

That was all he had meant about his responsibility.

'You never did anything to try and help when the car was burning?'

'I could not see if he was there, for one thing.'

'Do you swear that?'

'I swear that.'

Sergeant Skelly had been mistaken about him having seen

the man in the car, and having tried to rescue him.

Rouse could say nothing more about the unknown man, except that his breath had smelled of drink, although he was pressed to remember every detail.

'How many hats have you?' asked Mr Birkett. 'Several?'

'I have only one hat that I use for outdoor purposes. There is one hat I use for the garage, and one cap I have had in use for a long time; but I only use one hat in the ordinary course, a big Stetson hat, a very noticeable hat indeed.'

The jury no doubt noted this curious brag, just as they'd noted him say that 20 mph 'is very slow for me, because I usually go very fast, to be quite frank with you', in answer to one of Mr Marshall's questions.

This matter of travelling speed came up again soon afterwards, when Mr Birkett wanted to know how it had taken him so long to reach Markyate from London – a distance of 20 miles.

'Were you driving continuously?'

'Yes, but going quite slowly.'

'You told us today that when going twenty miles an hour you "went very slowly", and you ordinarily go much faster?'

'Yes.'

Rouse had, incidentally, already provided some proof of this on the insurance form that Mr Kennedy had read out; against a query about the applicant's driving record, he'd written: *Exceeding 20 miles per hour, otherwise licence not endorsed* – which gives one a better idea of what this particular speed meant in those days.

Even so, Mr Birkett could still say to him: 'I am putting it to you that a twenty-mile journey which takes two hours is absurd.'

'I do not admit it took two hours.'

'What time did you start?'

'I do not know. I did not see a clock.'

A dozen questions, each an attempt to fix the time of his departure from Buxted Road, ended with:

'Do you carry a watch?'

'No, never,' said Rouse, the commercial traveller, 'I haven't one.'

A passing mention of Buxted Road in another context needed sorting out – Rouse had, in fact, called there before catching the coach to Wales.

'When you said this morning, when giving your evidence about that, "To be honest, I went home," what did you mean?'

'I did not want at the time to bring my wife into it,' Rouse explained, 'and I went home. The police were bound to be inquiring about my car, as the number and everything was plain, and I did not want her to be upset, and I said, "I'll be back tomorrow." '

Mr Justice Avory asked: 'Why did you say "To be honest"?'

'I wanted to be frank. In the previous statement I had not said a word about going home.'

Rouse was pressed on why he hadn't disclosed this fact before and said, in effect, that it'd been purely and simply an omission.

It had still been dark on his arrival there around six a.m., and Mrs Rouse had been in bed. His stay had lasted anything up to half an hour, during which time he had not eaten anything nor changed his clothes.

'Your panic had gone then?'

'My panic had gone, but I was far from being composed. I was thinking about the whole thing; I was very upset indeed.'

Asked why he hadn't then contacted the police, Rouse replied: 'I made up my mind to carry out my arrangements first.'

The moment came for the Crown to move in on that small patch of Northamptonshire roadside which had been chosen as its battlefield. There would be further skirmishing to the south and in Wales, and some further sniping, also aimed at destroying any impression that the accused's conduct had been that of an innocent man, but the two major lines of attack lay at Hardingstone.

These were to use the evidence found there to prove: that the car had been burned by design – and that the position of the body was consistent with guilt.

'You drove continuously?' Mr Birkett repeated, beginning the advance.

'I did not stop the car, but I drove very slowly because I did not have the headlights on.'

Nor did he have them on, he said, as he approached Hardingstone and turned by mistake up the lane leading to the village, thinking he was still on the main road. He couldn't recall seeing a signpost at the corner.

As for the mallet, he might have used its handle to unscrew the cap on the petrol can, but he could not account for the thing being found fourteen yards away.

Rouse had, in fact, told Inspector Lawrence that the man might have used the mallet for the same purpose, and Mr Birkett asked him to explain this contradiction.

'He asked me a reason. I did not study the question carefully. I was asked for the answer to a riddle.'

'A *riddle*?'

'Yes, I did not know why the mallet was there.'

Again and again it wasn't so much what Rouse said, as how he expressed it, that disturbed those who feared an unjust conviction. Take this question-and-answer, for example, which has been extracted from among scores like it:

'A man in the car and not a human soul anywhere else – what did you walk 250 yards for to evacuate?'

'I should have done so in any case. I always do.'

He meant, of course, modesty mattered to him. But this gift for making almost anything sound absurd, if one can call it that, wasn't remotely funny in a man being tried for his life.

'I want to ask you a question or two about the Morris Minor and the petrol,' said Mr Birkett. 'You know a good deal about cars?'

'I have had a good many cars,' replied Rouse, and went on to explain that he'd built himself a garage in which he carried out minor repairs.

'You know all about the engine, and the petrol supply, and all the rest of it?'

'Yes.'

When it came to the quantity of petrol in the car itself, however, those one or two questions were multiplied, it seemed, endlessly. And the same happened with the petrol can. Put as yet another riddle, the problem came down to: When is a full tank not a full tank? – When a man says the tank he filled on November 5 was very nearly full, but then again, possibly it wasn't even nearly full, although it might have been, after he'd filled it.

What did eventually appear to be clear was: the tank held five gallons; the car did about 30 mpg; it had travelled approximately 100 miles since the 'fill-up'; there should have been, at the very least, one gallon left when the stop was made – if not two.

'Let me work that out,' said Rouse.

Mr Birkett went through the arithmetic involved and then observed:

'There was no need to fill up at all, was there?'

'I did not want to fill up at all, but the car had spat once or twice or several times, and I thought perhaps my estimation was wrong.'

Rouse said he'd had cars with leaking petrol unions, but he didn't think there had been a leak in the Morris, because it would have been 'smellable'. He also said quite straightforwardly, for once, that he understood the dangers of igniting petrol because he owned a blow-lamp.

But Colonel Buckle's theories about how the fire had spread under the bonnet were quite beyond him.

'Will you take that in your hand?' Mr Birkett said, nodding for Exhibit 45 to be passed up to the witness box.

Rouse blanched.

'That is the carburettor. Will you accept it for the moment that it is the carburettor from your car?'

'Yes, it is the same type.'

'Will you keep it in your hand for the moment,' murmured Mr Birkett, aware of a certain tension in the witness.

Which increased while he had him admit that if someone were to take the top off the carburettor, then they could ignite this source of petrol from the road.

'Yes, but you would get a flash in any case,' Rouse pointed out, using the right jargon, 'and a very bad flash indeed, with the amount of petrol in there.'

To clarify his meaning, he added: 'When I light the blow-lamp, I always do it with a rag.'

The defence counsel exchanged glances.

Rouse went on being helpful, encouraged in this by Mr Birkett, who said he wanted his opinion of suggestions concerning the carburettor which would be made to a defence expert witness.

Then Mr Birkett asked him: 'A flash from there would travel to the leaking joint inside the car?'

'I do not know. It is possible it would, but I do not know. That is too technical for me. You are talking about the travelling of fumes.'

'I will leave it,' Mr Birkett said quietly. 'It was because you introduced the word "flash" that I asked you; otherwise

I should not have asked you the question. You said "a flash" and, upon instructions, I put where the flash would go.'

In the momentary pause that followed, the Crown linked up its other line of attack and launched a barrage of accusations that had a remarkable effect.

Within less than two minutes, Rouse had delivered the second of his never-forgotten replies – one which was described as being the most sinister in the history of the courts.

'I am suggesting to you,' said Mr Birkett, in effect for the third time, 'that yours was the hand that fired that car.'

'It was not.'

'And that at the time you fired that car, your companion – picked up on the road – was unconscious.'

'No.'

'And that he had been thrown in that unconscious position, face forward, into the car that you were to light?'

'Most decidedly not,' Rouse retorted, in the tones of a man being belittled. 'I should not "throw" a man. If I did a thing like that, I should not throw him down face forwards.'

His indignation increased and he said: 'I should think where I put him, I imagine.'

There was a gasp from the onlookers in the gallery. Mr Justice Talbot turned sternly in his seat.

'You imagine what?' asked Mr Birkett.

'Hardly that I would throw him down like nothing. That is absurd.'

'If you rendered him unconscious, would you have a delicacy about his posture?'

'No, but I think if I had been going to do as you suggest, I should do a little more than that.'

'Would you?' Mr Birkett goaded him.

'I think,' Rouse replied, 'I have a little more brains than that!'

Which is where the trial ended for a great many people who were actually at it – although the prisoner still had some way to go before he completed his three hours in the witness box. And despite the fact that the whole of Friday was spent on more expert guesswork, both medical and technical, advanced by the defence.

Saturday dawned with leaden skies that were soon to bring

a blizzard raging about the Northampton County Hall. This had little deterrent effect on the huge crowd gathered outside, and the police had to erect barriers and call in mounted men to keep order.

Then, as the morning drew to a close, this crowd noticed that the Union Jack on the county hall flag-pole, weighed down by ice, had slid to half-mast.

And inside the building, two women in the public gallery used opera glasses to scrutinize what might prove to be the last public moments of Alfred Arthur Rouse.

Mr Justice Talbot's summing-up was painstakingly fair – the Lord Chief Justice was to call it masterly – and went on until after two.

Part of his advice to the jury was to start with the facts that *hadn't* been disputed, and he gave a very striking illustration of what he meant with some simple arithmetic.

Both sides had agreed to the measurement made between the car and the spot where Rouse had first been seen by the two cousins.

'To run that distance – 620 yards,' said Mr Justice Talbot, 'it would probably take a trained athlete on a racing track at least a minute and a half. A man like this, in ordinary clothes, on an ordinary road, it would take – even running as hard as he could – probably double that.'

The car had been blazing furiously when Rouse reached the end of the lane, and it was still blazing furiously when Brown and Bailey ran up – having themselves just covered 620 yards.

And yet, if one took the defence story as true, Rouse had run 970 yards from the moment the blaze began, and this estimate was based on minimal figures: 250 yards from where he evacuated back to the car; 50 yards towards the village; 50 yards back to the car; and 620 yards to the spot where the encounter had taken place.

By this reckoning, the flames had stayed leaping as high as 12–15 feet for at least a quarter of an hour.

If one took the prosecution's allegation as true – that Rouse had lit the fire and fled, in such haste he'd forgotten his hat – then the flames had stayed at 12–15 feet for about eight minutes.

This is one of those things which are so obvious, once someone has pointed them out, that it's easy to wonder why nobody had thought of it right at the start.

At 2.18 p.m. the jury retired.

Lily Rouse strained forward and her husband in the dock chucked himself under the chin, which was taken to be a gesture of cheerful reassurance.

'Only three Sundays left for me, I suppose,' he had said on his return to that dock after giving evidence – an allusion to the belief that three Sundays had to pass before a convicted murderer could be executed.

But now he was smiling.

The general opinion was, in fact, that the jury would have difficulty in reaching a unanimous verdict. When all was said and done, Mr Finnemore's persistent demand for some explanation that 'justified' the murder of the unknown man could not be ignored. And as the jury were being asked, in one sense, to kill a stranger themselves, they at least would want to have good reasons for doing so.

In practical terms, this suggested that there would be ample time for a leisurely if belated lunch, and the courtroom emptied rapidly.

Colonel Buckle undoubtedly spent some of the adjournment modestly recounting how he'd had the idea of having Mr Birkett press the carburettor on Rouse. It had come to him overnight, after thinking very carefully about the prisoner's attitude to his evidence about the leaking joint. Rouse had not seemed at all troubled by it, presumably because he knew that it was a fact that such joints commonly 'wept', and so the answer had to lie elsewhere. With three sources of petrol to choose from, and two of them virtually eliminated, the rest hadn't been very difficult.

But whether Colonel Buckle ever managed to finish his lunch is another matter.

Because word suddenly spread that the jury were about to return much sooner than expected, and people were seen bolting out of their hotels and running back through the sleet to the county hall. In a few minutes, the court was packed again.

At 3.33 p.m., after having had their lunch, and having inspected a Morris Minor, the jury filed in and answered to their names.

Then Mr Pleydell Bankcroft, the Clerk of Assize, put the

question that was on the tip of every tongue: 'Do you find the prisoner guilty, or not guilty of murder?'

'Guilty.'

And the verdict had been unanimous.

'Prisoner at the bar,' said Mr Bankcroft, turning round, 'you have been arraigned upon a charge of murder, and have placed yourself upon your country. That country has now found you guilty. Have you anything to say why judgement of death should not be pronounced upon you, and why you should not die according to the law?'

Rouse, looking 'slightly more concerned as usual', as one journalist described him, moved to the front of the dock and leaned with his hands on the rail.

'Only that I am innocent, sir,' he replied.

The death sentence was passed. The judge's hand fell heavily to his desk as the final words were uttered: '. . . and may God have mercy on your soul.'

'Amen,' said the chaplain.

But that wasn't all. Something else had to be settled before Rouse was hustled below, accompanied by his two warders, the prison doctor and the governor, all of whom had been with him in the dock for the verdict.

'My Lord,' said Mr Birkett, 'there was another indictment on the file. Would it be your lordship's pleasure that the indictment should remain on the file?'

'Yes.'

And that really was the end.

But it couldn't have pleased everyone; least of all the ladies with the opera glasses, who now trained them on three stunned and ashen women being helped to their feet. That shelved indictment had been for bigamy – an abrupt reminder the trial had, far from revealing all, only deepened the mystery of the hatless man and the Hardingstone murder.

Of course, while Rouse still lived, there was always the chance that somehow an explanation would be forthcoming.

One prevalent rumour was that he had, in fact, killed a man who'd been blackmailing him, and had refused to use this in his defence out of a sense of honour. An unlikely supposition in view of his blatant immorality, yet, in the midst of so much uncertainty, it couldn't be totally dismissed.

Then again there was that question of the £1,000 insurance

which a dead man could hardly have collected for himself. This implied someone else had to be involved, but the evidence, called by the prosecution at both hearings, had been left as a baffling 'blind spot' in the case and never commented upon.

It all seemed to depend on what the condemned man might do once his last hope of a reprieve had been dashed.

Mr Finnemore and Mr Marshall, who felt very strongly that the committal proceedings had made it impossible for Rouse to have a fair trial, went to work on that reprieve right away. They were assisted by Mr G. B. Lee-Roberts, his instructing solicitor, who'd fought hard for him from the start, and also believed in his innocence.

Many people didn't go quite so far as that, but they did have enough doubt in their minds to call for a reprieve as well. They were chiefly from among the newspaper-reading public, who'd had only the bare words to judge by, and then just a tiny fraction of the quarter of a million spoken over those six days. One cause of their unease was the way in which the police had handled the case – Mr Justice Talbot had said in his summing-up that he wouldn't have believed such negligence possible, if he hadn't heard it admitted by the officers themselves. Another cause was the way the expert evidence from either side tended to cancel itself out, particularly in a cramped column. Dr R. B. Harvey-Wyatt had, for example, given a plausible reason for supposing Sir Bernard was wrong about the body's position, and Mr H. W. Bamber, a consulting engineer with considerable experience in motor cases, said he'd heard nothing inconsistent with an accidental fire.

The grey days began to slip by more and more quickly.

On February 23, Rouse dressed himself appropriately in a dark suit and tie, and went under escort to London to have his appeal heard. Sir Patrick Hastings spoke eloquently on his behalf, but the appeal was rapidly dismissed.

The date for the execution was fixed: Tuesday, the tenth of March. There were, however, still a number of things Rouse's counsel could try that might spare his life.

While everyone waited to hear what these attempts would achieve, Mrs Jones – whom Bedford knew perfectly well was really poor Mrs Rouse – became a familiar figure as she went to and from the prison. Her red hair and the green hat she always wore made her easily recognizable even at a distance, and once, those passing close to her noted she'd just had a tooth extracted.

The month of March began.

On the fourth an application to appeal to the House of Lords was refused by the Attorney General.

On the sixth the Home Secretary refused to grant a reprieve.

On the seventh, or thereabouts, Rouse – surely without any hope left at all – asked someone to go on an errand for him. Until then he appears to have been his usual cheery self, and had spent a great deal of his time writing letters and snatches of his life. But when that someone returned, the prisoner went into a decline.

On Sunday the eighth the *News of the World* claimed that Rouse had confessed.

On the ninth the *Daily Express* counter-claimed that Mrs Rouse had denied this.

The ninth of March was also the day when 'this saintly woman' saw her husband for the last time. She spent nearly an hour in the visiting room at Bedford Prison, and at the conclusion of her stay, both she and Rouse kissed the bars which separated them.

'Goodbye, dear,' Rouse is alleged to have said, 'you are the best woman I have ever known. I hope the future will hold greater happiness for you.'

Her reply was: 'Poor, poor Daddy. You certainly don't deserve this. I will pray for you.'

And as the ninth became the tenth, Rouse dozed and sometimes moved restlessly about the condemned cell. He refused breakfast and was allowed to put on his own clothing; his choice was again the dark suit.

When the executioners, Tom Pierrepoint and his assistant Arthur Phillips, entered the cell, Rouse apparently said nothing but swayed and almost collapsed as they pinioned him. His short walk to the scaffold was made slowly and mechanically. Nonetheless, the Pierrepoint family always prided themselves in their swift methods of dispatch.

Within ten seconds, Alfred Arthur Rouse was dead.

No bell tolled, and there was a comparatively small crowd outside the prison gates when the notice of execution was posted. It must have been a drear and terrible morning for

Mr Finnemore and his colleagues.

Quite how they felt twenty-four hours later is impossible to imagine. That was when the following was published in the *Daily Sketch*.

'It was the Agnes Kesson case at Epsom in June which first set me thinking,' read the first line of Rouse's confession. 'It showed that it was possible to beat the police if you were careful enough.

'Since I read about that case I kept thinking of various plans. I tried to hit on something new. I did not want to do murder just for the sake of it.

'I was in a tangle in various ways. Nellie Tucker was expecting another child of which I would be the father and I was expecting to hear from 'Paddy' Jenkins similar news. There were other difficulties and I was fed up. I wanted to start afresh.

'I let the matter drop from my mind for a while, but in the autumn of last year something happened which made me think again.

'A man spoke to me near the Swan and Pyramid public-house in Whetstone High Road. He was a down-and-out, and told the usual hard-luck story. I took him into the public-house and he had some beer. I had lemonade. Of course, I paid for the drinks.

'He told me he usually hung about there. I met him once again and stood him a couple of drinks. He did not tell me his name, but he did say he had no relations, and was looking for work. He said he had been to Peterborough, Norwich, Hull, and other places trying to get work, and that he was in the habit of getting lifts on lorries.

'He was the sort of man no one would miss, and I thought he would suit the plan I had in mind. I worked out the whole thing in my mind, and as it was then early in November, I suddenly realized that I should do it on November 5, which was Bonfire Night, when a fire would not be noticed so much.

'I think it was on November 2 or 3 that I searched out the man. He was having a drink of beer and we talked. When I said I intended to go to Leicester on the Wednesday night, he said he would be glad of a lift up there. This is what I thought he would say.

'I made an appointment with him for the Wednesday night for about eight o'clock. I met him outside the Swan and

Pyramid, and we went into the bar. He had more beer, and I again had lemonade.

'I asked him if he would like something to drink on the journey, and he said he would. I bought a bottle of whisky. Then we both got into the car, which was outside the public-house.

'We drove first of all to my house in Buxted Road. I got out, leaving the man in the car.

'My wife was in. She had seen me draw up near the house and asked me who it was I had in the car. I said it was a man I knew, but she suspected it was a woman.

'I said, "All right. I'll drive close up in front of the house, as I am turning round, to let you see that it is a man."

'I did so, as I drove out of Buxted Road, so that my wife could see for herself and have no grounds for jealousy.

'So far as I remember, it was about 8.30 p.m. when I started off for the north with a man in the car, though I might be mistaken about the time. I drove slowly because I wanted it to be late when I did what I had in mind. I don't think I travelled more than fifteen miles an hour.

'I stopped at St Albans partly for a rest and partly to fill in the time. The man switched out the lights by mistake and a policeman spoke to me, as is already well known.

'During the journey the man drank the whisky neat from the bottle and was getting quite fuzzled. We talked a lot, but he did not tell me who he actually was. I did not care.

'I turned into Hardingstone Lane because it was quiet and near a main road, where I could get a lift from a lorry afterwards. I pulled the car up.

'The man was half-dozing–the effect of the whisky. I looked at him and then gripped him by the throat with my right hand. I pressed his head against the back of the seat. He slid down, his hat falling off. I saw he had a bald patch on the crown of his head.

'He just gurgled. I pressed his throat hard. My grip is very strong.

'I used my right hand only because it is very powerful. People have always said I have a terrific grip. He did not resist. It was all very sudden. The man did not realize what was happening. I pushed his face back. After making a peculiar noise, the man was silent and I thought he was dead or unconscious.

'Then I got out of the car, taking my attaché case, the can of petrol, and the mallet with me. I walked about ten yards in front of the car and opened the can, using the mallet to do so. I threw the mallet away and made a trail of petrol to the car. I took the mallet away with one purpose in view.

'Also I poured petrol over the man and loosened the petrol union joint and took off the top of the carburettor. I put the petrol can in the back of the car.

'I ran to the beginning of the petrol trail and put a match to it. The flame rushed to the car, which caught fire at once.

'Petrol was leaking from the bottom of the car. That was the petrol I had poured over the man and the petrol that was dripping from the union joint and carburettor.

'The fire was very quick, and the whole thing was a mass of flames in a few seconds. I ran away. I was running when I came near the two men, but I started to walk then. It is not true that I came out of the ditch when the men saw me. I was on the grass verge. I did shout to them that there must be a "bonfire over there."

'I did not expect to see anyone in the lane at that time of night. It surprised me and I decided to change my plans.

'I had intended to walk through to Northampton and to get a train to Scotland. But when the men saw me I hesitated and went the other way. The men were right when they said they saw me hesitate.

'I left my hat in the car. When I was driving, I nearly always did so with my hat off. I forgot, in the excitement, to take it out of the car.

'I went to Wales because I had to go somewhere and I did not know what to do. I did not think there would be much fuss in the papers about the thing, but pictures of the car with long accounts were published, and I left Wales.

'I was not going to Scotland, as I said. I just went back to London because I thought it was the best thing to do. London is big.

'In my attaché case was my (army) identity disc, which the police still have. I intended to put it on the man in the car so that people would think it was me. I forgot to do so.

'I knew that no one would find out that the man had been strangled, because the fire would be so fierce that no traces of that would be left.

'I am not able to give any more help regarding the man who

was burned in the car. I never asked his name. There was no reason why I should do so.'

And the following Sunday this letter appeared in the *News of the World*:

'I have fought to the last ditch to save my husband's life. But, alas, I have failed, and the law will take its course. Those who knew him well knew the good that was in Arthur. I did, so did others.

'But I knew I was fighting a lost cause, for before he went to the Court of Criminal Appeal he told me that the jury's verdict was the correct one and he was guilty. My own opinion is that he was not in his right mind on November 5th. Signed, Lily May Rouse.'

Dated: March 7 – the Saturday before his execution.

There is no question of the authenticity of Rouse's confession.

Moreover, it has his stamp all over it – only an extraordinary braggart would be unable to resist making the macabre boast 'People have always said I had a terrific grip'. It's almost as chilling as his final, throwaway remark, and, for those who recall the subject of his joke with the coach company manager, there's a small shudder in his having provided the doomed passenger with whisky. Read quickly, at the speed he might have delivered these words aloud, there is a suggestion, in his momentary asides, that he could well have begun: 'Unaccustomed as I am to confessing in public, I'd like to take this opportunity to rap a few knuckles . . .'

As to how much truth his confession contains, that is obviously another matter.

After a long and detailed description of the care taken to select the right man for his desperate scheme, which is convincing enough, Rouse then asserts that he drove this man home and made sure Mrs Rouse had a good look at him. Let alone any neighbours intrigued by his elaborate departing manoeuvre, and they can't all have been round the back at a fireworks party.

It's not only odd that apparently *nobody* should have recalled this happening, it's simply unbelievable that Rouse would have done such a thing. After all, his planned deception depended on one person being known to be in the car, and on one body being found in its ashes. (The fact he was undeterred to be seen with a passenger by a humble bobby at Markyate, who was polite and didn't take his number, is compatible with his contempt for provincial policemen.)

There are also significant omissions in this account of his preparations, but these can be left for the present. So can the probable reason he started his 'bonfire' so late on Bonfire Night that it was bound, paradoxically, to command the immediate attention of any wayfarer or insomniac, as it might on any other night.

The important thing to note is that where Rouse is *merely confirming* what the jury had presumably imagined for themselves, then he sticks to the truth. When he ventures into the 'unknown', it's up the garden path.

Even when one hasn't enough information to check out each point, the give-away comes when he quite blithely and openly contradicts himself near the end:

'I was not going to Scotland, as I said.'

Some may claim an ambiguity about this statement, yet it does seem curiously deliberate, it does tie in better with what went before than what follows, and it is very typical of the way Rouse edged towards being genuinely frank in so much of his evidence.

The absence of any repentance in a murderer's confession is also unusual enough to be worth pondering. This oversight might be construed as sheer callousness, or it might, just conceivably, be supposed that Rouse was unwilling to implicitly shoulder all the blame himself.

So, if Rouse still had no intention of telling the whole truth, then what was the point of him issuing this admission of guilt, as it were? What did it achieve? Especially when it denied Arthur Rouse Jnr, his adored and adoring son, the consolation of believing that the jury had been wrong. Surely no fee – charitably assuming that in some way his legal family was to benefit – would ever compensate for this. There are at least two answers that fit, but they would take an entire book to fully document, justify and explain.

Which doesn't mean, however, that a quick glimpse at the rest of the main pieces of the puzzle will go amiss. One could see this as placing fresh facts before a second jury. It's doubtful that the verdict will be unanimous, and, in the face of so many bizarre elements, some jurors may be content to settle for 'guilty, but insane'. What is certain is that, even in outline, the life history of this killer makes a most fascinating tale.

Alfred Arthur Rouse was born on April 6, 1894, to a respectable London hosier and a small-time Irish actress. In 1900 the marriage broke up, and the three children were sent to live with an aunt. Rouse never recovered from the loss of his mother, and often referred to it in his philanderer's patter, saying how he had yearned for her caresses. There is actually an echo of this in his 'harem' speech: 'I like a woman who will make a fuss of me.' He was six when this traumatic separation occurred – as was Arthur Junior when his father was hanged.

Stanley Bishop of the *Daily Express* once wrote that Rouse was 'at times the most cheerful murderer I have seen'. Perhaps he'd learned as a boy that cheerfulness under adversity was a quality ordinarily much admired by authority, because his school reports were warm with praise for his courage and brightness.

After leaving board school, Rouse served only a very short time as an office boy before skipping several rungs of the ladder to become a salesman in a West End soft-furnishing store. He remained there for five years, and spent his evenings on various 'improving' activities. These included learning the piano, violin and mandolin, how to make best use of his pleasant (if surprising) baritone voice, and some lessons in carpentry. He also courted an office girl, Miss Lily May Watkins, and found time to be a sacristan at St Saviour's Church, Stoke Newington. Mahon not quite all over again . . .

Just four days after the 1914–18 war began, Rouse volunteered for the army and began his training as Private 2011 in the 24th Queen's Territorial Regiment. And as Arthur, aged twenty, he married his Lily, aged twenty-three, at a church in St Albans on November 29 of the same year. On March 15, 1915, he was sent to France.

Rouse left behind him a portrait of himself in uniform that might well have been retouched by a Pre-Raphaelite artist, and yet is an accurate record of his appearance at the time. It shows a quiet, introspective-looking young man with unusually fine features and sensitive, intelligent eyes; exactly the sort of young man who would spend his leisure hours in the way described. As for the uniform, it suggests the costume of a juvenile lead in some sentimental production, and contributes nothing soldierly to the picture. If one places this portrait side by side with the equally solemn plate showing him in his thirties, the contrast is almost as striking as in the 'before and after' of a body recovered from the sea, or perhaps one which has been lying out in no-man's land too long.

That is not devious pacifism: it is fact. As it is a fact that on May 25, 1915, a shell exploded at Givenchy and ended the war for Private 2011.

This moment came as Rouse, already a veteran of some of the bitterest fighting, saw an aeroplane overhead collapsing in a ball of flame. He jumped up to look at it, and the shell splinters struck him in the temple and above the left knee. The next thing he remembered was being taken through a station which had 'Bedford' painted over its notice board.

Back in England, a cripple and in considerable pain at times, Rouse's gallant good humour encouraged the nurses to mother him. This much is on record, but it is reasonable to suppose that, once his condition improved, his good looks also attracted a little innocent flirtation. The combined effect these responses could have had on the sacristan-turned-atheist need not be spelt out. And the effect of spending his convalescence in a stately home – the magnificent Harewood House – will soon be obvious enough.

A lesser man might have opted to become a permanent invalid, but there was good in Arthur, as Lily May said. In August 1916, his disablement was assessed at 100 per cent and he was given a pension of 25s a week. By the autumn of 1920 he was entirely self-supporting.

Rouse worked hard as a commercial traveller and kept finding better homes for his wife and himself until, in about 1927, they took out a mortgage on the £750 house in Buxted Road. The neighbours grew used to seeing him either gardening or keeping the house in good repair – at what seemed like every available opportunity – and to his passion for motor cars. It appears his garage contained, according to a reporter who saw inside it, a 'remarkable set of tools' (the property was never officially searched).

Lily was his devoted servant, it is said, and was obsessed by the thought of keeping his collars and shirts in impeccable condition. Ironically, a word which couldn't really be over-used in this story, the defence was later to pin its hopes at one stage on fæcal matter being found on the tail of the shirt Rouse had worn on Bonfire Night.

His wife also saw to his book-keeping, and obliged the neighbours on occasions by cutting their hair.

Hindsight rather spoils any comments these neighbours had to make when the Press swooped down after the verdict, eager to put a bit of colour into their reports. Men were alleged to have found him an amusing companion but not a man to be trusted.

Other sources say Rouse soon became a popular figure, and nobody disputes that he was the life and soul of the local tennis club. At parties he was frequently called on to sing the hit songs of the day; his own favourite was, however, 'Trumpeter What Are You Sounding Now?' – and he'd follow this up with the 'Cobbler's Song' from *Chu Chin Chow*.

Rouse became the subject of a pseudo-popular song himself after his arrest, although it was sung chiefly by children in the street. Eddie Cantor had put 'Making Whooppee' into the equivalent of the charts, and its lyrics were reworded:

There was a man.
His name was Rouse.
He had the key
To every house.
He was suspected
And then arrested
   For making whooppee!

One wonders if this might have pleased Rouse had he known about it. One could also wonder at what the reaction of his audience might have been, had he disclosed to them how he learned the words of the new songs he sang.

They were copied down, as it happened, by the 'shadow' Mrs Rouse, a former Scots cotton mill worker who was now a waitress in London.

Helen Campbell was her name, and she believed that the real Mrs Rouse was her Arthur's mistress. Miss Campbell had fairly good grounds for assuming the truth of this, having been married to him at St Mary's Church, Islington, in November, 1924 – which does seem to be his month for decisive action, coincidence aside: two anniversaries and one murder.

But having moved behind the Buxted Road 'front', so to speak, it's best to leave 1927 and go back to when Rouse began to travel the country in his car. At least eighty seductions of impressionable young women were finally attributed to the dashing Major, a product of Eton and Cambridge, whose Mama was Something Rather Special in Society – the fantasies of Harewood House.

Yet if sexual experience had been Rouse's dominant interest, then the chances are that he would have died a natural death (unless cut down by a paternal shotgun), and the tennis club would have been there to let loose a volley over his grave.

Let him explain, using a fragment of one of those letters he wrote in his cell:

'My wife has always looked after me in every way possible and is very well domesticated, but that does not make up for the loss at the hearth of one's child . . . I honestly think that if I had only a child in my home all this trouble would never have come about.'

This also goes some way to explain his long relationship with Helen Campbell, which began in 1920 when, as a 15-year-old in the home of a friend, she bore Rouse a child. The infant died five weeks later, but their association continued until they were 'married' in 1924. Now feeling properly secure, Miss Campbell conceived again.

During this pregnancy, Rouse picked up a servant girl at Marble Arch, offered her the novelty of riding in a car, and took her out into the country where, it is stated, intimacy occurred. Seventeen-year-old Nellie Tucker, who had eyes everyone seemed to remark on, and an enormously jolly disposition, went on many journeys and joyrides after that. Including several with the boy born to Miss Campbell on July 22, 1925, as a second passenger. It isn't clear how Rouse explained him away; the real Mrs Rouse he passed off as his aunt, 'Old Toffy Face'. Nor is it clear how Miss Tucker came to know about her.

However, at last Rouse had an heir in Arthur Junior, and he was very happy for a while. In another part of the previously quoted letter, he said: 'I then realized what I had missed in life as regards my home.' As he'd already realized the need for a child, this must be a reference to his own childhood – he and Helen were doting parents.

To temporarily confuse the issue, Rouse admitted in prison to having fathered upwards of ten illegitimate children, among them one in Paris. But, as the women who bore these off-spring didn't seem to impress him much, it can be assumed that this somehow didn't count.

Miss Campbell must have impressed him. Despite her humble origins, the Edinburgh lass was canny, enterprising and, from what one can gather, Rouse's intellectual superior by a very long chalk. On the other hand, that may be a hasty judgement based on his performance at the trial, and she could have met a need in him for more than clean linen and a spot of slap and tickle. He used to play chess with her, and besides copying out songs, she would write scraps of verse on slips of paper for him to carry in his pockets.

In short, this woman probably came closer than anyone he knew to being the ideal mother of his dream child.

And, as ideal situations are wont to do, the 'marriage' came unstuck. Miss Campbell, who had been bringing in the lion's share of the family income, announced that she was going to take up a partnership in a restaurant. This challenged Rouse's patriarchal pride and there was such a row that they parted.

Nellie Tucker, promised marriage on a date never fixed, conceived and had a girl. Being fairly canny herself, she obtained a maintenance order against Rouse in 1928 and passed the child on to a foster-mother.

Then Helen Campbell was forced to obtain a maintenance order against him in 1929. At the hearing Rouse readily admitted paternity and spoke about his great interest in having children, which possibly surprised the case-hardened. But he was very irregular in his payments, and his ten-shilling postal orders were difficult to cash – he'd make them out to *Hell & Company*.

These maintenance orders resulted in the two Mrs Rouses – Lily and Helen – clashing in the parlour at Buxted Road. Lily won when she produced her 1914 marriage certificate, and the women came to an agreement that Arthur Junior should live under his father's roof. Mrs Rouse liked the child and treated him as best she could, even to the extent of having him sleep in his cot in the master bedroom, where he was on the night of the murder. (His mother took him back after the arrest, and he became a favourite in Fleet Street newsrooms.)

It is really rather incredible Rouse had managed to keep things a secret for as long as this. Although, of course, he'd had his women *wanting* to believe in him and everything he said, and he'd had another advantage in having a job which could be used to explain regular absences.

That winter must have depressed Rouse. Some attempt to lighten the gloom was made early in the brand-new year of 1930, and subsequently Miss Tucker disclosed that she was going to have a baby, probably in the first part of November.

That spring must have really shaken him. It was then that Rouse is said to have done something quite unprecedented: he fell in love.

What was almost certainly unprecedented about this final liaison is the fact that for once he involved himself, not with a lonely young woman with no one to care for her, but with an entire family.

More significantly, he soon began to plot a murder which would eventually mean the total destruction of the thing which symbolized a decade of decadent behaviour: his motor car.

While Miss Tucker had been becoming heavier with child, Rouse had taken to waiting about outside the door of a Highgate hospital from which the off-duty nurses emerged. He met 'Paddy', chatted her up, and they started taking drives in the Morris. This happened about four times a week, but there is good reason to suppose nothing unduly intimate occurred, because Rouse apparently recognized that this former Sunday School teacher was 'different'.

Paddy, who understood he was single, presumably thought the same of him, if in the romantic way young love draws its distinctions. She listened enrapt as he spoke of plans to emigrate to New Zealand or the South Sea Islands.

And then she invited him home to Primrose Villa in Gellygaer, delighted by the thought of showing him off to the family. Gellygaer, Rouse discovered, was a 'nowhere' place; Mr Cannell, the reporter, later claimed that on the two occasions he'd personally tried to reach it by taxi, his drivers had lost their way.

Rouse discovered as well that Paddy's father – her proper name was Ivy Muriel Jenkins – ran a small colliery, and would allow a new member of the family to buy a share in it; just a few hundred pounds would do. To a man who had about £3 in the bank when he was detained by Sergeant Skelly, that must still have sounded a great deal.

On Derby Night, Agnes Kesson, a 20-year-old blonde

waitress, was strangled at Epsom. On June 6, the papers were talking about the 'prospect of an early and sensational arrest'. The *Daily Sketch* of June 11 reported that Chief Constable Ashley had been going about in a 'high-powered car', and suggested that there would be 'dramatic developments'. The same story did, however, add that: 'At the moment the police are having a certain difficulty in connecting clues they have gathered . . .' Soon the public's interest in Miss Kesson was being kept going with such information as that her funeral had been paid a surprise visit by the Rev. John McNeill, whose intuition had led him to a 'poor Scottish lassie' in need of his blessing. Then a man somewhere else attacked Mary O'Connor in a clump of bushes and the Epsom strangling went on the spike.

Mr Jenkins started being addressed as 'Dad' by Rouse after Paddy returned with news of a quiet wedding on June 12; she had attended some sort of ceremony in a room with two men officiating. Mr Jenkins also started being impressed by Rouse, who promised that on November 6 he would be installing Paddy in a £1,250 house (which didn't exist) at Kingston-on-Thames.

Paddy's sister, Miss Phyllis Jenkins, who didn't trust her brother-in-law, was invited by him to join them at Kingston for the first three months – and she agreed.

During the autumn, the unfortunate Mrs Rouse proper, who had been consoling herself with a firm conviction that she was the woman her husband thought most highly of (and with visits to a Soho restaurant she insisted he took her on), found a photograph of Paddy Jenkins in his pocket. They began to discuss a separation.

At much the same time, Paddy told Arthur that she was expecting their first baby in March.

March is another month which seems to keep cropping up, but always as a period when Fate takes the upper hand: the trenches, an important birth, and an execution. Which is really far too glib: Paddy's baby was stillborn shortly before its sire was sentenced to death.

As a catalyst, however, the foetus had its part to play, and Paddy Jenkins returned home seriously ill because of her pregnancy late in October. Whereas on October 29, Miss Nellie Tucker gave birth to another daughter – and to a further problem for Rouse to solve: the maternity hospital in the City Road made a demand for *this* Mrs Rouse's marriage certificate.

The obvious solution was to have Nellie pretend that she was Helen Campbell; at least the 'date of birth' wouldn't be as noticeably ridiculous as the one on 38-year-old Lily's contract.

And the obvious place to get a copy of the bigamous certificate was at Somerset House.

Rouse didn't go there. Instead, on November 1, he went back to St Mary's in Islington and asked the clerk, Mr Turner, to help him. Possibly Mr Turner showed some sign of recognizing Rouse, who had been the third man he'd 'married' and so had remained in his memory.

Something must surely have prompted Rouse to explain to Mr Turner that he was, in fact, not Alfred Arthur but his brother.

Four days before the murder, Rouse went on, quite inexplicably, to tell Mr Turner that he was acting on behalf of his brother's widow – the reason being that A. A. Rouse had, most tragically, been burned to death in a terrible car accident.

Rouse's ruse worked on the hospital.

He was there at Miss Tucker's bedside at 7.10 p.m. on November the fifth to ask after her and the baby. But she noticed he seemed very depressed, and kept eyeing the clock. He left after an hour.

At nine there was a 'terrible row' at 14 Buxted Road, Arthur Junior is alleged to have told the police, which involved his father and 'Auntie Lil'. In an interview, Mrs Rouse explained that this row had been caused by her returning home later than expected that night, with the result that the preparations for her husband's departure were not complete until 9.30 p.m.

Then Rouse drove off into a night of dainty violence, in which rockets burst overhead like muted shells, and crackers rattled like small-arms fire among the shrubs of suburban London. He dawdled through the countryside, had a few words with a policeman, and moved on another 37 miles at a snail's pace, allowing the hours to drain away the main strength of a carefully calculated plot. Then, when it was really too late, he stopped short of a bend on a road half a mile long, and, within sight of some houses, carried out his mission. His nerve held while he adjusted the position of the victim so that both the face and bruised neck would be totally destroyed. But it may have broken when the car erupted into a ball of flame, and, at a glance, the land over the hedgerow suggested the muddy expanse of a battlefield in Flanders.

Which isn't entirely conjecture. It is based on what has been said to have brought about his collapse on the eve of his execution.

By then most people were agreed that Rouse's biggest mistake had been allowing himself to be seen by Brown and Bailey. If only he had hidden himself successfully, there would have been no 'hatless passer by' to make the main headlines.

And one theory was that Rouse had indeed ducked into the ditch at the approach of the car which passed the two cousins, but had missed the sound of their own approach in the roar of the retreating engine.

It appears, however, that Rouse had never intended to use Hardingstone Lane to reach the main road.

His idea had been to cut directly across the field beside the blazing car, which would have been by far the quickest and safest route to take. Only the field had looked to him as if it'd been ploughed up, and that he would leave tell-tale tracks in the mud, and so he had been forced to compromise by sticking to the verge.

Quite unnecessarily, as it turned out. And this was the message brought back to him from Hardingstone by that someone he'd sent from the prison to settle a sudden nagging doubt. The field hadn't been touched by a plough – his eyes must have played a trick on him, as he turned away from the dazzling brightness of the blaze.

From a blaze which had truly shocked and horrified the ex-soldier, to judge by the effect its recollection had on him in the box. That was when Rouse, who never expressed a single word of pity for the unknown man, had wept – and his manifest self-pity had disturbed and disgusted all those who witnessed it.

'What a fool I was,' he is alleged to have said on receipt of this information, his smile finally fading.

But just how much of a fool was Alfred Arthur Rouse? Was there nothing left in him of the courageous youngster who'd gone to fight in France? Not perhaps some kind of strange and twisted honour?

He wasn't such a fool that he failed to realize instantly what the consequences could be of his having been seen by the two cousins. Think about it.

And let Mrs Rouse provide a fitting epitaph for his unmarked grave. In one of her sad letters to Helen Campbell after the hanging, she wrote: 'Even Madame Tussaud's have an effigy.'

Chapter Four

THE CHALK PIT MURDER

REX *v*. THOMAS JOHN LEY AND LAWRENCE JOHN SMITH

MARCH, 1947

Originality is not something one looks for in murderers who get caught, as should be obvious enough by now. But at least each case usually offers novelty in its detail.

Rouse found an imitator in a London builder who, for twenty-four hours in 1933, succeeded in having someone else's charred body mistaken for his own. The builder's name was Mr Furnace. And he killed himself in a police cell with the bottle of hydrochloric acid he'd sewn into his overcoat.

Yet what does one make of this list of jottings taken not – as you might well suppose – from the Rouse case, but from the Chalk Pit Murder?

A Wednesday in November – mud underfoot – a road to a village from a main highway – two homeward-bound men coming across a curious stranger – a small car in strange circumstances – an unoffending victim – strangulation – a damp rag with an odour providing a clue – an accused who says he is driving up to Leicester – a teetotal accused who is sexually obsessed – no apparent motive for the killing – another 'Lil' – and, talking of names, a mysterious man in a woman's life whom she calls Arthur . . .

Probably that the Great Crime Writer in the Sky, having run out of fresh ideas, has finally gone to pieces – an assessment which isn't far wide of the mark if the intention is simply to suggest there's madness involved. No murder has even been madder, nor – in terms of its execution alone – badder. It was a thorough-going nightmare from which poor John McMain (call me Jack) Mudie never woke up.

It was also the end of an impossibly far-fetched story which had special features of its own.

When bees stung to death a magistrate in the Australian city of Perth in 1922, they made a merry widow of Maggie Evelyn Byron Brook, who was forty.

From the other side of the continent hastened someone she

had met the previous year at an official function: the Minister of Justice for New South Wales, the Hon. Thomas John Ley, a married man with a family. He added cash to his condolences, and then invited Mrs Brook and her daughter to live with him until they could get settled. Off they went.

Not everyone would have accepted his hospitality with such apparent alacrity. 'Lemonade Ley', abstainer and vegetarian, was an accomplished politician who did his job well, but there were – particularly in a man who weighed over twenty stone – other sides to him. He was disliked for his 'smarmy' manner, and for dumping dubious shares on his colleagues. He was feared for the inexplicable things which happened to those who crossed him. A rival candidate in an election, whom he was alleged to have bribed, vanished without trace before the High Court inquiry. Some years later a business associate was found dead at the bottom of some cliffs. And then there was something odd about a criminally-assaulted boy as well . . . one whose killer was released by Ley after only nineteen months in prison.

In short, although he lived on the other side of the world, this dishonest, fraudulent character was very much a contemporary of Messrs Mahon and Fox, and an Englishman to boot.

The Hon. Thomas had arrived in Australia at the age of eight in 1889; like Miss Helen Campbell's counsel, Mr S. R. Campion, he had begun as a newspaper seller before taking up law. Forty years on, exceedingly rich and – among other things – peeved at not having been made Deputy Premier, he returned to his mother country.

Mrs Brook and her daughter followed in his wake some months afterwards in 1930, and he bought the widow a house in Wimbledon. During the intervening eight years or so, he and Mrs Brook had been going places together: America, Canada and the Far East being among them.

Until roughly 1937 Mrs Brook was Ley's mistress and then sexual intercourse ceased between them and she was later reclassified as his housekeeper. While this signified a change on the physical plane, it didn't mean that the prohibitively gross Ley had lost interest in her. Far from it: he took her out to dinner every night with hardly an exception, and they would often play gin-rummy together. It could also be said – with rare accuracy – that he remained insanely jealous of his

Maggie, and this was the cause of the mayhem to follow.

The house in Wimbledon was let during the war, and Mrs Brook and her master moved into a Knightsbridge flat. When the lease ran out in the summer of 1946, Ley planned to take himself off to the National Liberal Club, and Mrs Brook, whose daughter had married a respectable young man, Arthur Barron, rented a room at 14 West Cromwell Road. This parting of their ways was an interim measure. Ley had bought the property at 5 Beaufort Gardens, a cul-de-sac behind Harrods, and was converting it into four self-contained flats, one of which Mrs Brook was to lease for a nominal sum.

Then the young Mrs Barron, née Brook, had to go into hospital for an operation – and the trouble began.

Ley suggested to Mrs Brook that she should move to her daughter's Wimbledon flat for several very sensible reasons. Mrs Brook would be near to the hospital for visiting; she would be more comfortable; she could help her son-in-law with running it; and she could contribute something towards the upkeep, thus helping her relatives at an expensive time in their lives.

Not unnaturally, Mrs Brook agreed to the idea, and arrived at 3 Homefield Road somewhere around the beginning of June. Her subsequent and sudden departure would, however, owe nothing to rational thinking.

The grey-brick Victorian villa belonged to Mrs Blanche Evans, who had three gentleman lodgers, as well as the Barron couple, living in her house. One of these lodgers, a quiet and unassuming Scots barman, reminded her of Bing Crosby. His name was Jack Mudie, and she had come to like him enormously.

One morning, while Mrs Brook was sweeping the stairs outside her daughter's flat, Mudie came out of his room and she met him for the first and last time.

Mrs Evans introduced them and they spoke about nothing in particular, the way polite strangers do, on the bathroom landing for five minutes. The nearest to a sordid affair they got was when Mrs Evans said that Mr Mudie was still a bachelor at 35, and Mrs Brook, aged 65, quipped: 'Well, he won't be for long with those beautiful blue eyes!'

That was all.

Only Ley can indicate the grounds for suspicion that

assailed him on June 8 when he called, as was his custom, to take Mrs Brook by bus for dinner at the Cumberland Grill.

'I arrived at the house rather early and walked in with someone who was under the impression that I was going to give her some surprise she would welcome.

'When I got to the top of the hall, I heard voices – her voice and another, a man's voice, both of whom seemed to be very happy, and she was calling him 'Arthur'. It was that name that registered in my mind.

'I went downstairs and closed the door, because I was quite satisfied from what I had heard that I was not wanted, and I pushed the bell ringing the electric bell in her flat.'

And now for the unforgettable . . .

'She put her head out of the window and she looked transfigured, very white, and said she was boiling an egg.'

Four days later, at about ten in the evening, Ley rang Mrs Brook and accused her of cohabiting with her son-in-law. Then at 2.30 a.m. he arrived in a hired Daimler and took her to the furnitureless flat in Knightsbridge. Mrs Brook, it is clear, was frightened of him.

Whereas Mrs Evans, the Wimbledon landlady, found Ley's person, his coarse remarks, and his great smacking kiss – applied as a form of greeting – quite repulsive. It did not please her at all when he called the following Sunday for an explanation of what had happened in her house to necessitate Mrs Brook's 2.30 a.m. removal.

Mrs Evans said she wasn't up at the time and didn't know.

So Ley told her that Mrs Brook had rung him up in a very great state of agitation, claiming all men were beasts, and that this had forced him to come to her rescue. Just what men were there in the house, Ley wanted to know.

Apart from Mr Barron, there was a Mr Arthur Romer, a Mr Wynn, and a barman at The Dog and Fox, with whom Mrs Brook had exchanged a few words on one occasion, Mr Jack Mudie.

'Jack,' echoed Ley, 'she is always mentioning his name.'

Then he heaved himself up and went away, planning – if that's not too ordinary a word – his terrible revenge.

Arthur Romer was invited to a meeting with Ley. Very much a family man, who went home every weekend to his wife and children, Mr Romer asked if he could bring his two brothers along. These brothers, his reply added, were both boxers. That ended their brief association.

Mr Barron was telephoned and invited to tea at 5 Beaufort Gardens by a woman who said she was his mother-in-law. 'It can't have been Mrs Brook,' he told his father, 'it must have been her maid – she spoke in a most uneducated voice.' Mr Barron Senior warned him to stay clear of Beaufort Gardens, and checked with Mrs Brook, who pointed out to him that she had been at 14 West Cromwell Road since the day after her precipitate move.

Jack Mudie received an astonishing piece of mail on June 20, which included this covering letter from the secretary of a property company:

Dear Sir,

Mrs Brook telephoned last afternoon that she was going to the country about some arrangements in regard to the convalescence of her daughter, who is still in hospital, and as we want some cheques signed and returned to us not later than Friday next, we asked for her instructions.

She directed us to send the cheques to her in your care with the request that, if she did not reach Homefield Road by 4 p.m. on Thursday, to ask you to be good enough to seal up the enclosed addressed envelope and post it to her new flat at 5 Beaufort Gardens, London SW7, so we can send up on Friday morning by taxi and obtain them.

We enclose a stamped envelope addressed to her and marked, as she directed, 'Strictly Private', her instructions being that we were not to open the envelope on any account until she returned on Friday morning. Thanking you in anticipation for your help in the matter.

We are (etc.)

Mrs Brook was indeed a director of the company – and so was T. J. Ley.

The bewildered Mudie handed the letter to the son-in-law and he, in turn, passed it on to canny Mr Barron Snr about a fortnight later. His reaction was to take the cheques down to the company and make the secretary sign a receipt for them on the spot.

About the same time, Ley called again on Mrs Evans and asked her to arrange an appointment with Mudie, who had

since found a better job in Reigate. Ley 'felt very sorry for h...
and wished to help him financially. Mrs Evans was flabber-
gasted when her visitor then went on to say that there had been
'high jinks' in the flat, and that Mrs Brook hadn't been able
to 'keep pace' with such erotic excess. Ley felt poor Mudie was
due an apology, as well as compensation, for having been
mixed up in the affair.

Ley appeared at the Reigate Hill Hotel on August 7 and
asked Mudie about the cheques. He then drove Mudie to Mr
Barron Snr in Wimbledon to check out his story, taking with
him a stray Australian as a witness to the proceedings. Ley
denied that the cheques had been received, and the argument
ended up in a solicitor's office. There Ley admitted to having
sent Mudie the cheques as part of a 'little private detective
work' of his own (presumably to prove that the barman and
Mrs Brook were keeping in touch).

Mr Barron last saw Ley on September 25. He was told that
his Arthur had been confused with some other Arthur, and that
Mrs Brook had been locked in a room for two hours with Mr
Romer on the night of the boiled egg.

It was laughable. Fortunately, however, Mr Barron had
never seen anything to amuse him in the behaviour of Thomas
John Ley. He was, after all, a welfare officer.

And had his son gone to tea at 5 Beaufort Gardens,
he would have found a gang of hired muscle waiting for
him.

The head porter of the Royal Hotel in Woburn Place knew
Mrs Ley well. She had been a resident for most of the war
years, and had left in a flurry for Australia only some months
before. Mr Joseph Minden had, as it happened, sent on two
trunks for her.

He also knew Ley by sight because Mrs Ley's husband
had called to take coffee with her almost every day of her
stay.

So when Mr Minden saw the familiar figure checking the
hotel letter rack towards the end of autumn, he was able to
place him straight away. Then something unexpected occurred:
instead of merely grunting a greeting as usual, Ley came up
and spoke to him.

'I want a man with a car,' Ley said, 'a man who can keep his
mouth shut.'

Mr Minden was to comment later: 'I thought it was a strange thing to ask, but as I knew Mr Ley had been, or was, a solicitor, it might be in pursuit of his duties, so I asked him straight away if it was legal, and he said it was.'

Ley added that such a man could earn a year's salary in a couple of weeks, and handed over a Kensington telephone number.

Mr Minden passed it on to John William Buckingham, a bespectacled, middle-aged ex-boxer with a cauliflower ear, who stood six feet two inches tall. He had deserted from the army after Dunkirk, and was running a small family motor firm specializing in car-hire, which depended on the hotel for much of its custom.

Buckingham rang the number and a meeting was arranged in the lounge of the Royal. There Ley told him that, as a retired solicitor, he'd come in contact with two ladies who were the victims of a blackmailer. If he liked, a Mr Larry Smith would fill him in on the background.

Lawrence John Smith had a meal with Buckingham and explained that a mother and daughter were being blackmailed by a man who'd seduced them in Wimbledon. His intention was 'to get something' on this man.

Smith was, in fact, the foreman supervising the work at 5 Beaufort Gardens. He earned £7 10s a week, impressed his Dulwich landlady as a 'decent, sensible' fellow, and yearned – as so many seem to have done – to emigrate to South Africa. (New Zealand was his second choice.)

Meeting after meeting followed. Ley confirmed Smith's story by describing the 2.30 a.m. rescue he'd had to stage. Then he declared there was enough evidence on this degenerate Jack Mudie to make him sign a confession. By this time, most of these 'legal' machinations were taking place in the squalor of Ley's makeshift arrangements at Beaufort Gardens, and he said that Mudie was to be brought there, tied up, and left with him for the required signature to be appended.

According to Buckingham, the ideas man, their first scheme went wrong in a quite unforeseeable kind of way.

This is what should have happened. Buckingham's twenty-one-year-old son, John William Jnr, was to disguise himself as a chauffeur and drive him down to the Reigate Hill Hotel. There the father would pretend drunkenness, the son would call on Mudie to assist in removing him to the family Wolseley

– and one blackmailer would be in the bag.

Then the Wolseley was stolen on the big night – although they were lucky enough to have it returned by the police the very next day.

When Ley heard about this plan, he made it clear that his knights errant would have to do far better than that. And so Buckingham came up with a more elaborate scenario which called for a leading lady.

He chose Lil Bruce, the sharp-faced brunette married to a bus driver friend of his, and took Smith to meet them in a pub called The Green Man. Mrs Bruce was told the story about the blackmail, and when she asked if the kidnapping was legal, was assured that Sir Edward Ley, a solicitor, would hardly be involved in it otherwise.

When they came to identifying the blackmailer, Mrs Bruce had the undoubted pleasure of knowing exactly whom they meant: only three weeks earlier, while on a drive with Mr and Mrs Buckingham, they'd stopped at the Reigate Hill Hotel for a quick drink.

For her part in these righteous endeavours, the cook-housekeeper was to play a Lady of Means with her foot on the soft pedal. All she had to do was visit the hotel, see if Mudie spoke to her, and then – when the moment was right – ask him up to a party in London as part-guest, mostly cocktail-shaker.

Both Buckinghams escorted Mrs Bruce down there, and John William Jnr, in his peaked cap and mackintosh, went with her into the bar. She and Mudie got talking.

This was on or about Saturday, November 24.

Mrs Bruce appeared again at the hotel within a couple of days. This time she told Mudie about a cocktail party she was planning, and obtained his telephone number.

On the Monday of the following week, Ley had a car-hire firm bring a black Ford 8, registered as FGP 101, round to Beaufort Gardens to be rented for a week by Mr Smith, his site foreman.

On the Thursday, this Ford and the Wolseley set off in convoy for Reigate; Buckingham and Smith rode in FGP 101, and Mrs Bruce and her 'chauffeur', John William Jnr, in the other. Mudie was waiting on the hotel forecourt, all spruced up and with a new hair cut. Under his overcoat he wore a blue 'demob' suit in a broad chalk-stripe.

Which couldn't have been more grotesquely appropriate.

Back they all went to the dead-end street in London. For some of the way, Buckingham and Smith tailed along behind, and then they drove ahead to pilot the 'chauffeur', who didn't know the route too well nearer the metropolis. This gave them a small lead, just sufficient for their purpose.

The Ford went to the front entrance of 5 Beaufort Gardens, and the Wolseley to the back, where the basement door had a sign beside it, erected by Ley: THE OLD AIR RAID SHELTER. This was probably the last thing Mudie ever read, and it may have puzzled him as he alighted from the car.

What happened next, happened in the dark and happened quickly. It not only bewildered, it was terrifying.

Mrs Bruce handed a key to John William Jnr, who let her into the unlit house, followed by Mudie. But they had hardly crossed the threshold, when she said: 'Excuse me, I want to speak to John' – and went out again, closing the door behind her.

Mudie took a few uncertain paces.

Smith grabbed him around the body, pinning his arms, and said: 'All right, put it over!'

This was Buckingham's cue. He emerged from a recess, threw a blanket over Mudie, and restrained him while Smith went to work with a clothes-line bought that morning.

'You're stifling me!' the startled Mudie protested.

'You're breathing your last,' said Buckingham.

And then, when Mudie was trussed up, he 'jumped' him down the passage to the office where Ley was waiting.

In fact, it was barely five minutes after journey's end that Buckingham rejoined his son and Mrs Bruce in a pub across the way. Smith, he explained, had been detained pending the arrival of some other people, and would be going on to drive to Leicester. As for Ley, he'd said not to get in touch for a while. Buckingham gave Mrs Bruce £30 from his £200 fee for services rendered, and the three of them began a pub-crawl.

During which someone must have remarked gleefully on how easy it had all been. And to think that Mudie had himself picked November 28 for the party, saying he'd be off duty and free to do as he liked that particular evening.

Two days later and about twenty miles away, squeamish

Walter Coombs was skirting a chalk pit on his way home from work at about four. It lay beside the Slines Oak Road, which connected the village of Woldingham to the main Croydon highway, and was, at that time of year, a bleak and rather unpleasant place.

Mr Coombs found something which did not bear close examination and went to fetch his father. The elder Mr Coombs lifted a chalk-stripe trouser leg to see what was beneath it, and then went to fetch the police.

The body, in a blue demob suit, was lying on its right side in what looked like the remains of an army field latrine, they observed. This trench was about eighteen inches across and twelve inches deep; although some attempt had been made to deepen it, probably with the pick-axe lying nearby, the dead man's feet were sticking out over the edge.

He had his overcoat pulled over his head, and a piece of rope had been wound round it twice, before being tied in two loose half-hitches. The coat was removed and the rope was seen to carry on around the neck – which was also encircled by a piece of green rag, and deeply marked.

The rag was damp and smelled of french polish.

Other details were duly noted. The soles of the shoes were perfectly clean, despite all the mud about, and smears of clay on the clothing confirmed the body had been dragged there. It had also been trussed up and then the rope had been cut to allow it to lie flat.

John McMain Mudie had been dead about 48 hours, said the pathologist.

Providing, of course, that the name on the visiting card left in his pocket was the right one; this discovery must have seemed almost too good to be true.

On Monday, December 1, the police were at Reigate Hill Hotel, some twelve miles from the chalk pit, and there they found two very curious solicitor's letters threatening legal action over some unreturned cheques. These proved to have been written on the instructions of a company director, Thomas J. Ley.

And on the same day, a couple of landscape gardeners saw a story about the chalk-pit body in the local paper, and this set them thinking.

Clifford Tamplin and Frederick Smith shared the same employer and the same route home. Late the previous

Wednesday, while pushing their bicycles up Slines Oak Road past the entrance to the chalk pit, they had noticed an incongruous figure.

The man had been standing on a bank on the far side of the pit, looking over in their direction. They had paused and looked back, idly curious to know what anyone would want there. To their amazement, the man had reacted by bolting down the bank and jumping into a small, dark car parked behind some bushes. He had revved the engine wildly, stalled it, and had made several attempts to reverse out before finally reaching the road. Where they'd caught only a glimpse of him as he shot by.

Mr Smith thought the car had been a Ford 8 or 10, and Mr Tamplin felt it could equally have been an Austin. But the one thing they both agreed on was its easily remembered index number: 101.

At an identity parade held in Brixton Prison on January 13, 1947, Mr Smith touched the shoulder of an innocent man. Mr Tamplin, however, put the finger on Lawrence John Smith, who'd hotly deny he had been anywhere near the chalk pit on the day *before* Jack Mudie was murdered.

And for very obvious reasons.

Mrs Blanche Evans, the musical landlady who gave piano recitals for the blind, had been mistaken about the young bachelor whose bedsitter she tidied every day, and with whom she occasionally had tea.

At the start of the four-day trial at the Old Bailey, a deposition by Mr Joseph Mudie was read out. The Scots plumber said he'd identified his brother's body, and that Jack had been a married man with one child.

It was Wednesday, March 19, 1947. The Lord Chief Justice, Lord Goddard, presided; Mr E. Anthony Hawke led for the Crown. Ley had Sir William Monckton, KC, for his senior counsel, and Smith had Mr Derek Curtis-Bennett, KC–whose father had departed this life in a remarkable way. 'I feel this is the last time I shall speak in public,' the well-loved Sir Henry had said, rising to his feet at a dinner of the Greyhound Racing Society; he made a good joke about his girth, paused during the laughter, and dropped dead.

Ley, who once could have more than rivalled him in size, was now a white-haired, distinguished-looking shadow of his former self as he sat there in the dock. He had lost his 'vast adipose deposit', according to Miss Tennyson Jesse, who witnessed the trial, and appeared to her quite 'normal' – if only in this one respect. As for Smith, he was an unimpressive little man.

Buckingham was not in the dock because, after being charged with the murder as well, he'd turned King's evidence. His son and Mrs Bruce were also to be called by the prosecution, but all three of them – plus Ley's secretary, Miss Ingleson – would not be paid witness expenses: a decision of some significance on the part of Lord Goddard.

A french polisher identified the green rag as one he'd used at 5 Beaufort Gardens, and two workmen did the same for the pick-axe.

'The mucous membrane of all the intestines was so congested that it looked like crimson velvet,' said Dr Eric Gardner, an old friend of Spilsbury's, and the pathologist who'd performed the post-mortem.

Although the external marking on the body had been relatively slight, the internal injuries he'd found 'suggested a thoroughly rough house'.

Mudie had died slowly, strangled by only 'some degree of suspension' – as though he had sagged against the pull of a rope running over the back of a chair. If the green rag had been used as a gag, then this would indeed have contributed to the asphyxia which killed him.

All because of a small, frail and timorous widow who had been taken about in buses, and who now rode to court in a hired Rolls Royce. Mrs Brook very definitely looked her age, Miss Tennyson Jesse decided, as the next witness took the oath.

'That, you say, is the only time you saw him?' asked Mr Hawke, referring to the meeting with Mudie on the landing.

'That is the only time I saw him ever,' replied Mrs Brook, who wasn't often adamant about things.

'Mrs Brook, did you first get to know Ley in about 1921 or 1922, when your husband was still alive?' said Sir Walter Monckton, beginning his cross-examination.

'My husband died 24 years ago, if you reckon that back,' she replied. 'I couldn't. I am sorry.'

Time and place were repeatedly shown not to be her strong points, and suggested that Mrs Brook lived largely in a world of her own.

But she did remember having tea with Ley at 5 Beaufort Gardens on the afternoon of November 28, because that had been the one and only day he hadn't taken her out to dine. Instead, Ley had arrived at her rented room at about 7.45 p.m., eaten sandwiches and played gin-rummy, and then had left again around eleven.

Lord Goddard thought she ought to be able to recall her reactions to Ley's accusations about Mudie trying to get money from her. She must, for example, have asked for his sources of information.

'Is that not what any woman would do – or any man, as far as that goes?'

'Well, I think we did argue and argue and argue about it.'

Pressed further about the accusation concerning improper conduct with her son-in-law, Mrs Brook said: 'I remember him saying once that he could bring five people forward to prove it, and I said, "Well bring five people forward. I would like to face them." That's all I can remember about it.'

Apart from this episode, she and Ley had been happy together. And she'd never accused him of Mudie's murder.

But there was a touch of spirit just before she left the witness box. Mr Hawke asked if she'd told anyone that she could account for Ley's movements on the night.

'Oh no, I didn't!' replied Mrs Brook.

Then stepped back into obscurity, taking the young Barrons to live with her in the original Wimbledon house.

'Well, I done it,' said John William Buckingham, when asked whether he'd been willing to carry out the kidnapping.

As simple as that.

Mudie had shown no resistance whatsoever after having the blanket thrown over him. He had been frog-marched to the office and sat in a chair.

'Was any violence done to this man,' said Mr Hawke, 'apart from what you have already told us?'

'None whatsoever.'

'Then you had got the man where you had been told to put him?'

'Yes. I took the blanket off his head; I folded the blanket right off his head before I left.'

Ley had handed him the balance of his £200, and he'd not seen the retired solicitor again. A meeting with Smith had, however, taken place the following Tuesday.

'Did he say anything about this affair to you?'

'Yes; the expression he used was: the old man was very pleased with the way things had gone, Mudie had signed a confession and was given £500 and got out of the country.'

By air – or so Buckingham had been led to believe.

Smith had then explained that, after waiting about ten minutes for Ley's friends to arrive, he'd gone over to the pub just too late to catch the party. He hadn't, in the event, driven up to see his estranged wife and family in Leicester that night, but had returned to his lodgings and made the trip on Friday.

Buckingham's first inkling of catastrophe had come about ten days later, when Smith called on him again.

'He said that Mudie was missing – and I took it he was out of the country – and that I wasn't to communicate with Ley; that was all.'

Then a picture-story had been published in the *Daily Mail* and, after talking to his son and Mrs Bruce, Buckingham had gone to Scotland Yard the same day, December 14.

His first statement had been a pack of lies– as Sir Walter Monckton lost no time in reminding him at the start of a brief cross-examination.

Which came to a close with: 'I put it to you that there is not a word of truth in your suggestion that Ley was there on that night, or that he made these preparations with you before.'

Buckingham emphatically denied this, just as he'd denied putting a gag in Mudie's mouth.

Mr Curtis-Bennett asked him: 'There was never any suggestion – apart from tying him up – that any violence should be done to Mudie, was there?'

'No, none whatever,' confirmed Buckingham. 'That was insisted upon – that there was no violence.'

'Who by?'

'Well, Mr Ley suggested we were to use no violence whatever.'

These two sets of questions and answers highlight two aspects of this murder trial, one of them quite bizarre, which make it very different to the others.

For a start, there is the obvious complication posed by having more than one person in the dock. Each accused comes under attack not only by the prosecution, but by the other accused's counsel as well. This has, of course, its reciprocal advantages, and here Mr Curtis-Bennett was cashing in on them for Smith.

But what was Sir Walter up to? Having failed to convince Ley that he should plead 'guilty but insane', Sir Walter was simply doing his utmost in a virtually impossible situation – the sort Mr Cassels would have faced had Mahon claimed to have met Miss Kaye in a strictly business capacity, once and once only.

That was, in effect, Ley's story and he was sticking to it.

Thomas John Ley was introduced to the jury as a former Minister of Justice, of Public Instruction, and of Labour and Industry. None of which titles would have seemed particularly apposite to those who knew him, except perhaps the latter, but they made it fractionally easier to pursue his chosen line of defence than if he'd been a travelling salesman.

The case against him sounded incredible because it *was* incredible and not a word of it could possibly be believed.

Ley told the court that the only contact he'd ever had with Mudie had been over the cheques, and that they had met just once to get it sorted out.

He had never mentioned Mudie to Smith or to Buckingham; he had never dicussed with them the details of Mrs Brook's private life; and he had not given them permission to use his premises on November 28. Nor had he spoken to the hotel porter except to give him a tip from Mrs Ley.

Sir Walter Monckton asked him if he'd formed an intimate association with Mrs Brook after her arrival from Australia, and if they'd lived in various flats and hotels together.

'Yes; but I would wish, Sir Walter, in view of the allegations that have been made about my insane jealousy, and my suspicions of improper conduct by Mrs Brook, and the suggestion that I am obsessed with her being blackmailed, to make a short statement, if I may, because I think my lord and the jury ought to have the background of what happened.'

Lord Goddard told Ley to just answer the questions put to him. And ticked him off again shortly afterwards for 'rambling on'.

Ley explained that the origin of the trouble concerning Mrs Brook had been the conversation he'd overheard while she was in the flat with 'Arthur'.

'By this time I understood you to say this lady had ceased

to be your mistress?' queried Lord Goddard.

'Yes; but I was not concerned on that account, and that is why I wanted to make it quite clear. I was not jealous about this thing. She had a perfect right to do what she wanted to do.'

The 'Arthur' intimacies he'd overheard had been unprintable – being uttered during sexual intercourse. She had told him on the telephone that she was 'packing up' and – when the literal meaning of this had occurred to him – he'd hastened to pick her up. Mrs Brook had been unable to sit down for four days.

'I tried to find out from Arthur Barron what could have happened, and he was very rude to me, as a matter of fact. I tried to get him along under conditions where he would listen to me, talk, and give information.'

To this end, Ley had paid some workmen to stay behind after hours at 5 Beaufort Gardens.

Mr Curtis-Bennett asked him: 'There were three people – apparently you were seeking – Arthur Barron, Arthur Romer and Jack Mudie?'

'No, I was not seeking Jack Mudie at all.'

And Ley added: 'I often wondered about Jack Mudie, whom I understood from Mrs Evans was a nice man.'

Mrs Brook had also, Ley disclosed, ceased to be his housekeeper in July after he'd discovered her dishonestly trying to claim a property for her own. Nonetheless, he had maintained an interest in her finances and welfare which still persisted; it had been their practice to have lunch, tea and dinner together.

After tea on November 28, he had left Mrs Brook to catch a bus, and then had taken a taxi to his club. He'd collected letters from his wife and a son in Hong Kong, and had dined at the Cumberland, quite forgetting that Mrs Brook should have been there, too. They'd had a date at seven.

'I remembered it when the coffee came along, and I got a bit excited and I left then.'

Sir Walter said: 'Did you tell her you'd forgotten the arrangement?'

'Yes; it was not the first time I'd done it, and I did not want to be teased about it.'

Ley conducted himself with an easy confidence in the witness box, as befitted a man of his former profession, and even attempted some dry, forensic wit.

When Mr Hawke was cross-examining him about £450 in cash, which Ley said he'd drawn out to pay for furnishings, and not to pay Buckingham and Smith, he was asked if there was any proof of this transaction.

'There are receipts about, but for three months I have been isolated from my business.'

'You have been in the best of hands?'

'Well,' said Ley, 'I would be quite willing to change places with you.'

It didn't seem likely that anyone could top Ley for an utterly astonishing performance under oath, but an ex-convict called on his behalf did just that. In fact, he set the mind reeling.

Robert J. Cruikshank's story was difficult to follow, being filled with dark hints and obsequious allusions, but this much became as clear as it could ever be.

The ex-convict had left his family in a Swiss hotel at 4 p.m. on November 28, and had flown in an 'unauthorized plane' to London with a smuggled package. Having some time on his hands before the return flight, he'd decided to go and see if Ley, whom he knew to be a rich compatriot, would help him with a passage back to Australia. The house at 5 Beaufort Gardens had been in darkness at eight o'clock, and nobody had answered to his knock. So the smuggler had turned his mind to burglary, entering the basement by the open side door. After stumbling along the passage, he had found somebody gagged and bound in a room.

'I was in a state of panic when I got into the basement, and I didn't know whether to believe my eyes or what to believe, and I stood for a couple of moments, and I heard some sort of moan or a grunt.

'I think I stood there for a couple of moments, and then went over and started pulling at some ropes.'

'*What* did you do?' said Lord Goddard.

'I just pulled at them, sir, in a sort of a frenzy.'

There had been a grunt from the bound figure, Cruikshank's nerve had snapped, and he'd been back in Switzerland for breakfast.

'Are you coming here to confess you killed this man?' Lord Goddard said.

'Oh no; but if there was a possibility, if he was bound in such a way – I can't say how it was done.'

Cruikshank concluded his evidence by revealing that he'd made a clean breast of his crimes to Scotland Yard, and said that by coming forward he had laid himself open to half a dozen charges. Oh yes; and once he had shaken hands with Mr Ley's son.

'Was that before or after you came forward to make your statement?' inquired Sir Walter Monckton.

'Afterwards. Thank you, sir. I apologize if I have said anything wrong, sir.'

And with that, the amazing Robert J. Cruikshank stepped down.

Lawrence John Smith's repetitive use of the words *actually* and *definitely* caused many of his listeners acute irritation. By now the absurdities of the case were wearing a bit thin, like a black comedy sketch that'd been allowed to go on far too long, and fools weren't being suffered gladly.

However, he was in the box for less than half the time Ley had spent in it, and for only a little longer than Cruikshank.

His story of the kidnapping corroborated most of what Buckingham had said, but differed in three major points of detail. Buckingham had fallen on Mudie while frog-marching him to the office, Smith claimed, and it had been Buckingham who put the gag on the hapless prisoner. Furthermore, Smith had known in advance that Ley wanted Mudie tied *and* gagged.

Mr Curtis-Bennett was able to achieve a good deal for him by bringing out how similar his role had been to that played by Buckingham, against whom the murder charge had been dropped, but this could be taken only so far.

There was, for example, the £300 which Ley had placed in Smith's bank account on December 4, making his 'cut' appear to have been £500, rather than the flat £200 he alleged they'd both been paid. Smith said the £300 had been a loan for a car which he hadn't needed after all, so he had paid it back again on December 9. As the jury knew, the police had been to see Ley between those dates.

Smith's demeanour was no help either, particularly when Mr Hawke was cross-examining him about what had happened while Mudie was being trussed up.

'And he said, according to you: "You're stifling me"?'
'Yes.'

'And the answer he got to that was: "You are breathing your last"?'

'That was only said in joking form,' replied Smith with a smile.

'Tremendously funny, do you think?'

'Well, it was done – '

'You seem to think it was,' said Mr Hawke, who asked Smith a little later on: 'So far as you were concerned, he was in no condition to make a confession either verbally or in writing?'

'When he was bound, as I said in my statement, his right arm was not bound.'

Now the jury had a much clearer picture: Smith had left Mudie, uninjured and with a hand free, to wait in the office while he and Ley had enjoyed a ten-minute chat before his dismissal. But why, in the name of reason, hadn't Mudie used that hand to release himself?

Smith could be as clever as he liked, and introduce all sorts of different shades of meaning, different versions of other people's stories, and a totally different conclusion to be drawn from his actions – but the one thing he couldn't do much about was the hired Ford FGP 101.

Asked what he'd intended to do with it, he said: 'Nothing particular at all, actually.'

'Were you not, towards the end of the week?' prompted Mr Curtis-Bennett.

'At the end of the week I was definitely going to Leicester for the weekend.'

No, he had not been to the chalk pit near Woldingham, and whoever's car it was that Mr Tamplin and Mr Smith had seen, it hadn't been his. Yet he couldn't produce any positive proof of his whereabouts during that part of the afternoon.

Nor of exactly where he had been between seven and 10.30 p.m. on the night of Mudie's murder.

And this made all the difference between something that had gone horribly wrongly and something that had gone according to plan.

The jury retired at 4.35 p.m. on Saturday, March 22, and were back in three minutes under the hour. Which could have surprised only those silly enough to call this, as some people still do, a 'baffling and motiveless' murder. If anything, it was an all-too-straightforward murder; and as for motivation, Mudie's guilt had been a 'psychic reality' to Ley, and Smith had badly wanted the money.

Both accused were found guilty.

Before the death sentence was passed, Ley made a pompous little speech, ending up with: '. . . and I regret very much that I, at my time of life, have to suffer an injustice of this kind that is utterly unfounded and based on anything but real fact.'

Smith said nothing.

Their appeals were turned down exactly a month later – one of the appeal court judges being Mr Justice Cassels.

But they didn't hang. Ley was found to be paranoid and became – so it was said – the richest prisoner ever sent to Broadmoor, where it was possible for him to have a private room and an inmate for a servant. As only seemed fair, Smith then had his sentence commuted to one of life imprisonment. Buckingham, by the way, also went to prison – for desertion.

There is just one more thing to add. On July 24 that year Thomas John Ley, the monstrous man brought to book by Chief Inspector Arthur Philpott, had a seizure in Broadmoor and dropped dead.

Chapter Five

THE STEINIE MORRISON CASE

REX *v.* STEINIE MORRISON, ALIAS ALEXANDER PETROPAV-
LOFF, MORRIS STEIN, STANLEY MORRIS. MOSES TAGGER,
MORRIS TAGGER ETC.

MARCH, 1911

It is just possible that Steinie Morrison[1] could still be alive
today if, among other things, his defending counsel hadn't
believed so passionately in his innocence.

For an example of a trial in illuminating contrast to the four
which have gone before, we leave 1947 – the year Sir Bernard
Spilsbury, ill and stricken by the tragic deaths of his sons,
killed himself – and travel back to the last days of 1910.

A new kind of criminal was abroad. The Tsarist police had
been deporting dissidents known as 'anarchists', and some
of them had come to live among the émigré Jews in London's
East End. These anarchists did not commit crime for vulgar
gain, but for the Cause – a morality with which we are once
again all too familiar. To get funds for distributing their
propaganda, they would stop at nothing – including walls and
ceilings, and that most heinous of crimes, shooting down
unarmed policemen.

On the night of December 16, a gang of them were boring
their way through from 11 Exchange Buildings into a jeweller's
shop at 119 Houndsditch. A neighbour heard the noise and
called the police.

Seven officers investigated. The gang shot one dead, fatally
wounded two others, dropped the rest – and accidentally
put a bullet into their own leader as well. Then they escaped
with him through the midnight streets of Whitechapel.

The Houndsditch Murders brought a tremendous public
outcry, and a man-hunt started throughout the land, with
'Peter the Painter' high on the wanted list. The injured gang
leader died and some arrests followed, but that was far from
the end of the affair.

At about 8.10 a.m. on New Year's Day, 1911, the body of a

[1] Thames Television favours 'Stinie Morrison' as this was the spelling
used in the Press reports of the time.

47-year-old Russian Jew, Leon Beron, was found in some bushes on Clapham Common. He had been beaten savagely on the head and stabbed, but his fatal injuries attracted less attention than did the superficial slashes on his face.

Two of these were taken to resemble the letter 'S' and this, in turn, was thought by some to stand for 'sckpick', the Russian word for spy, or variations on that theme. Beron had, after all, been living in Jubilee Street, Stepney, where the anarchists' club had stood.

Only a halfpenny was found on the man who'd died during the first three hours or so of that world-shattering decade.

The next day came a tip-off that two of the wanted anarchists were hiding on the second floor of 100 Sidney Street. By dawn on January 3, the police had ingeniously extricated a woman hostage, and had the place surrounded. Some gravel was tossed up at the window.

Rifles responded. The notorious Siege of Sidney Street had begun and a police sergeant lay bleeding. The Scots Guards arrived on the scene, and so did the Home Secretary, Mr Winston Churchill, and firing went on until one p.m. Then the house caught alight and the two anarchists were left to fry in it. Nonetheless, they claimed one more innocent victim, when part of the building collapsed on some firemen.

Such behaviour wasn't simply atrocious – it was alien to the whole way of British life as most Britons understood it.

Five days later the police arrested Steinie Morrison, 30, a Russian Jew who'd been in the country for over twelve years, and subsequently charged him with the S-marks murder.

The reason given for his arrest was that, as a convict on parole, Morrison had changed his address without informing them as he was meant to do. Five officers, led by the chief inspector in charge of the Houndsditch case, took him into custody. They thought he might be armed.

Now what have we here – one story or two?

The case, as presented by the Crown, was quite straightforward. Widower Leon Beron, a landlord believed to carry at least £20 about with him, had been taken to Clapham Common after midnight on January 1, and there murdered and robbed.

Beron, a Russian Jew, had lived nearly all his life in France before arriving in the East End in 1894. Although he owned nine small houses, Beron had resided in a rented room in a 'very poor way', spending most of each day in the Warsaw Restaurant, run by Mr Alexander Snelwar.

This Mr Snelwar had obliged Leon Beron by giving him gold coin for the silver presumably paid as rent. The gold was kept in a wash-leather purse, which Beron fastened inside his waistcoat pocket with a safety pin.

The deceased's other valuables had been a gold watch and chain, embellished by a captive £5 gold piece.

The accused, Steinie Morrison, a traveller in cheap jewellery, had formed a sudden friendship with Beron a fortnight or so before the murder, and they had spent most of December 31 together in the Warsaw, where 1s 6d would pay for three meals and beverages. That evening Morrison had asked the waiter to look after a parcel which he said contained a flute, but which the waiter judged to be a bar or iron. Then at 11.40 p.m., the accused had reclaimed his parcel and left with Beron.

The two men had been seen here and there together in the East End until about two a.m. This was when a hansom cab had picked them up at the corner of Sidney Street and taken them six miles to a theatre near Clapham Common, arriving at 2.38 a.m. or thereabouts. Ten minutes' walk away was the spot where the body had been found.

Another eleven minutes further on was the Clapham Cross rank, where the accused had hired a cab at about 3.15 a.m. This had taken him to Kennington, where he'd hired a third cab to take him to Finsbury Park – only by now he'd been joined by another man.

On New Year's Day Morrison had put his nose into the Warsaw Restaurant, and then gone away, never to return again. That same morning he had left a loaded revolver and 44 rounds in a station cloakroom, after giving the clerk a false name.

He had then disappeared from the places he normally frequented. He had communicated with no one after the news of his companion's murder was bruited about. He had said: 'You have charged me with murder' – before the police had mentioned the murder to him. He had pawned a watch on December 23, but on January 1 he'd been well in funds. Except for that vital half-hour between the first and second cab ride, his movements were known.

The bloodstains found on his shirt collar and cuffs at the time of his arrest also suggested that he had committed the murder, although why he was wearing the same shirt a week later couldn't be explained.

These were the central facts of the case, the jury were told, and they didn't in the least depend on such things as bloodstains.

The defence had a straightforward reply that went something like this.

Steinie Morrison had not been a particular friend of the deceased, but had merely exchanged hello's and how-are-you's when they chanced to meet in the Warsaw. He didn't even know his name.

On December 31 Morrison had taken his dinner in the restaurant and left his flute there – with a waiter with whom he'd had a row – to visit a music hall. He had returned for the flute after the performance, seen Beron talking to a tall man on the corner of Sidney Street while on his way home, called out a greeting, and gone to his lodgings. The Zimmermans, his landlord and landlady, were certain he had not left the house again until the following morning.

On New Year's Day, he had arranged to live with a woman at a different address which made the Warsaw less convenient as an eating place, and had deposited the revolver for fear of alarming his new amour. The revolver was, by the way, just an article he had for sale.

As for his sudden wealth, there wasn't anything sudden about it at all. The money had been sent to him before Christmas by his old mother in Russia.

The stained collar was one he could prove having bought after January 4, and it had been marked because he was subject to nose bleeds – two prison warders could testify to this.

Furthermore, Morrison had been arrested with £14 on him; this sum would have been sufficient to get him out of the country, had that been his wish, in the hue and cry which followed the discovery of the body.

But instead he had gone about his business as usual, and the only part of his routine which had changed was that relating to his move to 116 York Road, and the bed of Florrie Dellow. A stone's throw of difference, in fact, if only someone had taken the trouble to look.

Matched one against the other like this, the Crown case

would seem to have far greater credibility – especially as all Morrison could offer with regard to that 'vital half-hour' was the Zimmermans' belief he was asleep on the couch in their front room at the time – a belief based on the dreadful noises the door and window made when anyone tried to open them.

Yet the vital part of the Crown case was really the evidence of those who swore to having seen him in Beron's company after midnight, and in particular that of the three cab drivers.

Their testimony was at once the strongest and the weakest link in the chain of circumstance the police had forged, because if ever evidence of identification could have a hansom cab driven through it, sideways, this was it.

On top of which, Morrison's improved fortunes had still to be proved, beyond a reasonable doubt, the product of a dastardly deed.

There were, however, to be some dizzying complications when the matter actually came to trial.

One of these was unavoidable. The twelve solid citizens who made up the jury found themselves trying to make judgements concerning a world they knew little, if anything, about. Not only was it alien to them – with all that word implied at the time – but they must have found it almost beyond belief.

Steinie Morrison himself gave an indication of the basic gap when talking about his skill as a burglar: '. . . the inhabitants of gentlemen's houses generally lived upstairs, there is nobody below . . . but you could not do it in a house in the East End though, where people are living in every room.'

And he turned the gap into a yawning chasm by stating, in a quite matter-of-fact way: 'Frank was in the kitchen with his wife and children having breakfast. This would be between twelve and one . . . I was taken upstairs by Mr Frank and introduced to Florrie Dellow. It was arranged between her and me that I should live with her.'

Just like that. And *breakfast*, did he say?

It was a world where motives and values on even the most ordinary level were nearly incomprehensible. Where some people worked endless hours and others not at all. Where the residents of doss-houses wore gold watches and dressed very comfortably. Where a restaurateur was content to have people sitting at his tables for twelve hours at a stretch, day in and day out, because he knew they had nowhere else to go.

Where these customers would look at their gold watches every ten minutes or so, and go right on sitting there. Where people would drift in from the four corners of the earth, including lone children from Galicia and hard cases from the States, all with – yes, one thing at least in common with the perpetrators of those abominable murders, there was no disputing it. One could be distracted by hearing that the Japanese Sanitary Laundry was also run by Russian Jews . . . but not for long.

And not when Mr Edward Abinger, Morrison's senior counsel, was on his feet having another bitter clash with the judge.

A judge who did everything in his power to ensure that the trial, which he personally felt could have been prejudiced before it began, was scrupulously fair. He treated the immigrant witnesses, in particular, with patience and due respect, while watching, clearly with some despair, the ambivalent Mr Abinger mock, taunt and jeer in a very complicated effort to secure Morrison's acquittal – which might otherwise have followed naturally.

Much has been made of the amusingly insolent replies this gentleman had directed at him during the trial: replies which have been held to epitomize the rare and delightfully un-inhibited characters who emerged from the shadows to give the occasion colour, unusual fascination and life.

But if the remarks which provoked these replies are given some attention, then it becomes immediately obvious that Mr Abinger was only getting back as good as he gave. These were the sort of spirited replies any one of us might make if subjected to gratuitous ridicule in a foreign court. In fact, a nastier display of racial bigotry would be difficult to find, encompassing as it did the notion that all foreign males are idiots and crooks, and that their womenfolk are all whores.

Whether there was some truth in these insinuations in this specific case is beside the point, when one considers what Mr Abinger might have achieved with a cold politeness. Certainly the jury wouldn't have been as likely to start feeling indignant on behalf of the underdog.

The irony is that it possibly hurt Mr Abinger to do this. He was, after all, defending one of the very same group of people, and doing this up to the hilt. And he was, in some instances, acting on Morrison's instructions.

As for the further complication which lay behind his whole approach, this became apparent a very short time after the trial began.

On Monday March 6, 1911, Steinie Morrison, a tall, handsome man in a green suit, took up a stance in the dock at the Old Bailey, hand on hip. He declined an invitation to be seated, and stayed, standing proudly, for the whole nine days.

The pathologist said it was his opinion that Leon Beron had been killed at about three a.m. by eight blows to the head with a heavy instrument like a jemmy, and then had been stabbed three times in the chest. He could not express an opinion about the seven cuts on the face, two of which, having penetrated just the outer skin, resembled an S-shape.

Mr Abinger tried the same question on the doctor who'd seen the body *in situ*, and this time it paid off. These S's, said the doctor, who also compared them to the *f*-holes in a violin, could not have been produced accidentally. They could only have been made by design. Moreover, this was an objective opinion, as the doctor knew no Russian.

There it was then. Although the Crown had not linked the murder with the anarchists in any way, Mr Abinger was intent on doing just that. He not only believed Morrison was innocent, but that the man was being framed.

It must then have been an overwhelming sense of outrage, boosted by lies admitted in the lower court, and alleged death threats to a witness, that drove him on to such extremes.

Some were plain embarrassing, as when he said that Morrison would undergo an ordeal more terrible than the heretics 'in the days of the Inquisition' at the hands of Mr R. D. Muir, the dignified Scot leading for the Crown. To rub this in, he added that the contest would be 'as unequal as a fight between a professional prize-fighter and a curate'.

And some were dangerous, the judge warned him; dangerous to the prisoner – and he'd really better not.

But Mr Abinger went right ahead and became, in his way, the man this trial was really all about.

Now for a quick experiment that anyone can conduct in the privacy of his own bathroom – providing you have no objection to washing your face.

Take something that draws easily – a fibre-tip pen is ideal – and stand in front of the mirror. Touch the pen to your cheek next to your nose, and move your hand in a straight line towards your jaw, missing your mouth. Repeat for the other side. If you don't finish up with symmetrical lines 'extraordinarily like two S's', then you deserve the price of this book back. Not that there's much chance of any claims being made, because the 'bump' of the cheekbone will put a curve into the line, no matter how straight your hand moves. One other thing: don't be disappointed if the S isn't as pronounced as you would imagine. It wasn't on Leon Beron's face either.

Which proves? Well, perhaps that Mr Abinger would have been wiser to stick to the point.

Solomon Beron, high-cheeked, dapper and touchy, nearly halved the Crown's estimate when he said that his brother had been carrying only £12, and that the watch, chain and coin were worth about £30 in all.

Mr Abinger could have flattered him into admitting an expert eye for the value of second-hand goods, but he didn't.

Mr Beron said that he'd last seen his brother standing alone in the street at 10.45 p.m., and although he'd tried to speak to him, he had got no reply.

Mr Abinger could have used this to his advantage, by simply allowing it to lie uneasily beside the vital evidence of the Warsaw's waiter, who said Morrison and Leon Beron had been together all evening. He did not.

Instead, Mr Abinger made fun of Solomon Beron, and traded heavily on the witness's poor command of English.

'Do you describe yourself as an independent gentleman?'

'Yes.'

'Living in a Rowton House at 6d – I beg your pardon, 7d – a night?'

'What is that to do with the case?' Mr Beron demanded indignantly. 'It is nothing to do with the case. If you ask me independent [impudent?] questions, nothing meeting with the crime, I will not answer you!'

Goading him, laughing at him and attacking his credibility, Mr Abinger made much of the erstwhile travelling salesman's apparent affluence, and asked him if he'd met Peter the Painter. He also wanted to know if Solomon Beron had threatened a potential witness. These questions brought

181

denials, but the insinuations had been made nonetheless.

This is not to say that Mr Abinger ignored totally the case as it stood, and he worked hard on the three cab drivers, whose recollections of Morrison on that moonless, cloudy night, were unusually detailed, and those of his companion, notably vague.

Edward Hayman had gone to the police on January 9, which was the day that pictures of Morrison began to appear in the papers. He couldn't give any reason for delaying in making his report, but denied having ever seen the first picture, and said that the identification he'd made on January 17 had not been influenced, as he didn't 'go by portraits'.

Mr Hayman believed he'd taken Morrison to Clapham – Mr Andrew Stephens swore he'd taken him to Kennington. This witness had gone to the police on January 10, after seeing a police appeal, and after seeing Morrison's portrait that morning. He, too, had picked Morrison out of a line-up of Englishmen on January 17 – a fortnight after the papers had said that two foreigners were being sought by the police. But most vulnerable was the change he'd made in his estimate of when Morrison had boarded his cab at Clapham Cross: the first time he'd given conflicted entirely with Hayman's evidence and the second tied in very neatly. Mr Stephens was unable to say what had initially made him review his estimate, yet swore he had done so independently.

Furthest from the scene of the crime had been Alfred Castlin, who said he'd picked up the accused at Kennington Church at 3.30 a.m. Morrison and his companion had spoken in a foreign tongue, and this had taken him to the police on January 4, after he'd seen something about two Frenchmen in the paper. He had identified Morrison on January 9, before the first picture had appeared in the paper, from among a line-up of Englishmen.

Each of these cab drivers could have been telling the truth, and none of them need have been in any way affected by the Press coverage. What they had done unconsciously was, of course, another matter – and one to be exploited.

But Mr Abinger went and muddied the issue by asking Mr Castlin if he remembered the anarchist outrage that had been committed somewhere near where he'd dropped his fares in Seven Sisters Road. A man had jumped from a bus and shot some people, said Mr Abinger, and Mr Castlin agreed he knew about it.

The judge asked: 'When was this anarchist outrage? Was it before or after you took these men?'

'It might be two years previous to that,' said Mr Castlin. By now, however, the real damage had been done. The Criminal Evidence Act of 1898, which had permitted the prisoner to give evidence on his own behalf, had something of a Catch-22 to it. Very fairly, no questions could be put to him that would reveal previous bad character . . . *but* if the defence imputed the character of a prosecution witness, then it became a free-for-all. It wasn't a just law, yet it was the one under which the frustrated Mr Abinger was working.

His first warning of danger ahead came from the judge when Joe Mintz, the Warsaw waiter, was asked if he'd once tried to hang himself. Attempted suicide was a misdemeanour, the judge pointed out, and so this was an attack on the witness. Mr Abinger just managed to escape that time.

Then came the evidence of Mrs Nellie Deitch, a woman who'd been friends with Leon Beron for twelve years. She told the court that, while on her way back from a New Year party, she had seen Leon in the street with the accused – someone she'd never come across before. It had been after two a.m. She had gone to the police as soon as she'd heard about the murder.

Mrs Deitch was obviously a biased witness, and her evidence offered a good deal of scope for reasonable doubt to be conjured up. Mr Abinger struck hardest at her character, with the intent of showing that this so-called respectable mother of five ran a brothel.

'Where did you get that fur from?' he asked.

'That is my business.'

'Tell us, please.'

'Why should I tell you?' Mrs Deitch snapped back. 'You don't think I'm as foolish as all that! You insulted me last time, but you'll not insult me today. You asked me last time where I got my fur from: my husband bought it – what he worked for!'

Then she added: 'I do not ask you where *your* wife got her fur from!'

That certainly livened things up. So did the parade of shady ladies brought before Mrs Deitch to see if she knew any one of them: Dolly Nevy, Lena Hall, Becky Blue . . .

'Do *I* know you?' she scoffed at Sarah Lask.

'Yes.'

'How dare you,' stormed Mrs Deitch, 'come and tell lies?'

And much the same could be said of her as well, to judge by some of the things Mr Abinger achieved. But in a trial that prompted this sighed comment from the Bench: 'What is the use of looking at one liar more or less?' – it tended to drive the jury back on to the evidence of those cabmen, stolid Englishmen all, if a little slow on the uptake.

Worst of all, though, it permitted Mr Muir to reel off Steinie Morrison's previous convictions: theft, 1898; being a suspicious person on enclosed premises, 1899; burglary, 1899; possessing stolen goods, 1900; burglary (five years), 1901; suspicious person, having housebreaking tools in possession, 1906.

The prisoner had, in fact, been released on parole only the previous September.

Mr Abinger was furious and got into a lengthy wrangle with the judge when told that this was permissible because of his attack on the character of Mrs Deitch. He said that the Act was being misinterpreted, and read aloud from the relevant section.

'You left out "or witnesses for the prosecution",' the judge quietly rebuked him, as this was the really relevant bit.

'My lord, it was a slip,' said Mr Abinger.

Scrupulous fairness was, of course, something that had to be seen to work both ways .

The open season on Steinie Morrison continued. Mr Muir produced a letter which the prisoner had written to a previous Home Secretary while in jail, petitioning to be sent back to Russia. Morrison, who claimed to have been born in Sydney, Australia, admitted it was dishonest.

'Then, for your own purposes, and in order to deceive the Home Secretary, did you say that your name was Alexander Petropavloff, that you were born in 1879 at Korsovsk, a station in the district of Liutzin, in the Government of Vitebsk, in Russia?'

'I said that because I have had such bad luck here in England,' Morrison replied. 'Ever since I came to England, I've had nothing but trouble, and I tried to better myself for all that. Even here in England I have done my best to work honestly for my living, until I have been hounded out by these police officers.'

After leaving jail in September he'd worked as a baker's roundsman – working from a shop in the same area as he was alleged to have been dropped off to walk to Clapham Common. (This Crown line that he'd been familiar with the district still didn't begin to explain how he could have coaxed a sober Beron into going there in the small hours of the morning.)

Morrison said he'd bought the revolver cheaply in a shop and had hoped to make a profit on it.

'Why did you use a false name?' asked Mr Muir, referring to the station cloakroom ticket.

'Because it was a revolver, that was the reason.'

A fairly typical response from this imposing young man, whose warmth of personality is evident even in the cold print of the trial record; a bachelor who bought fruit for children, had an eye for a pretty girl, and who could observe social differences most wryly. A liar, too, when it suited him – and that seemed to go for his witnesses, too.

Mr Muir tested him at length on every point of the prosecution's case. There was the failure to comment on Beron's death, for example. But Morrison said he'd known him only as 'the landlord', and that the headline on January 2, *THE MAD LANDLORD*, hadn't meant anything, as the man he knew was quite sane. And then Mr Muir left it at that.

Before leaving the box, Mr Abinger had Morrison repeat that he'd never been accused of an act of violence.

In his astonishing closing speech for the defence, Mr Abinger pointed out that the prosecution had made no attempt to link the murder of Beron with the Houndsditch murders – and he defied them to do so.

Mr Abinger felt it was difficult to believe that a mere robber would pause to cut S's into the face of his victim. He suggested that Leon Beron could have been a police informer, and that his death might then be related to the fact of Peter the Painter still being at large.

He also felt it difficult to believe that Leon Beron, a Russian Jew, would have been eating ham sandwiches on the sly on the Sabbath, and punned: '. . . rather a large order to swallow.' Mr Abinger was questioning Beron's alleged movements after leaving the Warsaw, and the evidence of his having obtained a ham sandwich somewhere, although no ham had been found on him. But it had; there'd been evidence to that effect, which he had forgotten.

He lamented Mr Muir's use of the petition, and was told a better topic for lament was that the Home Secretary hadn't allowed Morrison to return to Russia.

Then Mr Abinger, who drew constant interruptions from the judge for the things he said, lauched into what he called a quiet, intellectual, dispassionate discussion. It was, in fact, a hypothesis which encouraged the jury to look around for someone besides Morrison who had a motive of gain for the murder.

'Take, for instance, Solomon Beron,' he suggested.

Before the jury heard the end of that speech, Solomon Beron had been removed to a lunatic asylum, where he eventually died, for having bodily attacked Mr Abinger. That must have been the most memorable thing about it.

The message in the judge's summing-up was never loud but it was clear; a reasonable doubt of Morrison's guilt existed.

'The fact a man calls false evidence, calls false witnesses,' he said, 'does not necessarily or by a long way prove he is guilty.'

Allowances had to be made for the ways of foreigners. In India, for example, even if the accused had a good case, he would feel obliged to bring perjured evidence – to counteract the perjured evidence being brought against him.

The judge 'deeply regretted' that pictures of the accused had been published while Morrison was being held merely on suspicion. 'It may have frustrated the whole ends of justice,' he remarked, and urged a change in the law to put an end to the practice.

What, the judge asked, was a 'medium complexion'? And made it obvious that evidence of identification was a very tricky matter.

The deciding point, it seemed to him, was Morrison's alibi – which seemed a surprisingly naive one for a guilty man.

And in commenting on the revolver, he cautioned the jury: 'You must not convict a man on one suspicion; you must not convict him on a thousand suspicions; you must not add a thousand suspicions together and say "that is proof".'

*

It took the jury under 35 minutes to find the prisoner guilty of murder, just as they might have done in a straightforward case. The death sentence followed automatically; but the judge pointedly left out his personal endorsement of their verdict, and made a comment that indicated Morrison should appeal.

At the beginning of his trial, Steinie Morrison had said: 'My lord, if I was standing before the Almighty, I could give but one answer. I am not guilty.'

. . . *and may the Lord have mercy on your soul.*

'I decline such mercy!' retorted the man now branded a killer. 'I do not believe in a God in Heaven either!'

A decided change in outlook which proved to be more than idle rhetoric.

His appeal was dismissed a week later. When there was sufficient evidence for a conviction, and the jury had decided the prisoner was guilty, there was nothing the courts could do about it.

And then on April 12, Winston Churchill signed his reprieve and Morrison was jailed for life.

While in Paris on the same day, an English lady overheard two men expressing concern that 'Stein' should hang for a crime he'd not committed. But the pair decided that their comrade 'Gort' – or 'Cort' – had to be protected, and elected to take no action. Nothing came of a police inquiry, yet the story couldn't be dismissed as a total fiction: other names she supplied belonged to an international gang, and were startling coming from a gentlewoman who knew about the case only from occasional headlines.

It was only one of several pieces of information pursued to no useful purpose by poor Mr Abinger.

Right up till the moment of his own untimely death, Steinie Morrison would keep protesting his innocence. Or rather the innocence of the man who'd stepped into the dock at the Old Bailey, because Steinie Morrison was no longer the same person.

After his reprieve, he became an unmanageable prisoner in Dartmoor, where his sense of outrage led to repeated acts of violence, and then he withdrew into a deep depression on being transferred to Parkhurst.

Four times he petitioned to be hanged rather than go on living, so they say. And when these pleas went ignored, he finally began a series of fasts that wore down his constitution and killed him.

That was in 1921, the year in which Patrick Herbert Mahon was released from a sentence imposed on him by the same judge, Mr Justice Darling: who went on, as Lord Darling, to react strongly over the effect newspapers had on the fate of Alfred Arthur Rouse.

He also went on to advocate the restriction of Press coverage during the preliminary stages of a 'sensational trial'; not a popular suggestion at the time, but a law we have in force before every trial today.

SELECT BIBLIOGRAPHY

The Trial of Patrick Mahon, introduction by Edgar Wallace, Geoffrey Bles (no date)

Trial of Sidney Harry Fox, edited by F. Tennyson Jesse, William Hodge & Co., 1934

Trial of Alfred Arthur Rouse, edited by Helena Normanton, William Hodge & Co., 1931

The Trial of Alfred Arthur Rouse, edited by Sydney Tremayne, Geoffrey Bles, 1931

Trial of Ley and Smith, edited by F. Tennyson Jesse, William Hodge & Co., 1947

Trial of Steinie Morrison, edited by H. Fletcher Morton, William Hodge & Co., 1922

Norman Birkett, by H. Montgomery Hyde, Hamish Hamilton, 1964

'*Curtis*', by Ronald Wild and Derek Curtis-Bennett, 1937

Bernard Spilsbury, by Douglas G. Browne and E. V. Tullett, Harrap, 1951

Encyclopaedia of Murder, by Colin Wilson and Pat Pitman, Arthur Barker, 1961

Dead Men Tell Tales, by Jurgen Thorwald, Thames & Hudson, 1966

New Light on the Rouse Case, by J. C. Cannell, John Long, 1931

Executioner: Pierrepoint, by Albert Pierrepoint, Harrap, 1975

Cautionary Verses, by H. Belloc, Duckworth, 1940

The Essentials of Forensic Medicine, by Cyril John Polson, Pergamon Press, 1964

Glaister's Medical Jurisprudence and Toxicology, edited by Edgar Rentoul and Hamilton Smith, Churchill Livingstone, 1973

Ross Macdonald

'Classify him how you will, he is one of the best American novelists now operating . . . all he does is keep on getting better.' *New York Times Book Review*. 'Ross Macdonald must be ranked high among American thriller-writters. His evocations of scenes and people are as sharp as those of Raymond Chandler.' *Times Literary Supplement*. 'Lew Archer is, by a long chalk, the best private eye in the business.' *Sunday Times*

Sleeping Beauty

The Way Some People Die

The Galton Case

Black Money

Find a Victim

The Barbarous Coast

The Drowning Pool

The Ivory Grin

 Fontana Books

Agatha Christie

The most popular and prolific writer of detective fiction ever known, her intricately plotted whodunits are enjoyed by armchair crime-solvers everywhere.

They Do It With Mirrors
Hercule Poirot's Christmas
Elephants Can Remember
The Hound of Death
The Murder of Roger Ackroyd
Mrs McGinty's Dead
Cards on the Table

After the Funeral
Murder on the Orient Express
The Sittaford Mystery
Endless Night
Nemesis
Passenger to Frankfurt
Hickory Dickory Dock
The Clocks

and many others

Agatha Christie is also the author of novels of romance and suspense under the name

Mary Westmacott

Absent in the Spring

The Burden
Giant's Bread

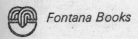 *Fontana Books*

Fontana Books

Fontana is a leading paperback publisher of fiction and non-fiction, with authors ranging from Alistair MacLean, Agatha Christie and Desmond Bagley to Solzhenitsyn and Pasternak, from Gerald Durrell and Joy Adamson to the famous Modern Masters series.

In addition to a wide-ranging collection of internationally popular writers of fiction, Fontana also has an outstanding reputation for history, natural history, military history, psychology, psychiatry, politics, economics, religion and the social sciences.

All Fontana books are available at your bookshop or newsagent; or can be ordered direct. Just fill in the form and list the titles you want.
